EXPLORING

~ AND ~

INTERPRETING

DREAMS

EXPLORING

~ AND ~

INTERPRETING

DREAMS

BENNY THOMAS

WHITAKER
HOUSE

EXPLORING AND INTERPRETING DREAMS

(Previously published as *Exploring the World of Dreams.*)

Benny Thomas
5355 Concord Road
Beaumont, TX 77708

ISBN: 978-1-60374-829-2
eBook ISBN: 978-1-60374-830-8
Printed in the United States of America
© 1990, 2013 by Whitaker House

Whitaker House
1030 Hunt Valley Circle
New Kensington, PA 15068
www.whitakerhouse.com

Library of Congress Cataloging-in-Publication Data (Pending)

This book has been printed digitally and produced in a standard specification in order to ensure its continuing availability.

CONTENTS

ACKNOWLEDGMENTS

My deepest gratitude goes to my wife Sandy who has faithfully stood with me during the development and writing of this book. She helped, encouraged, and sacrificed to see the manuscript completed.

I appreciate Susan, Anita, and LaRue, members of my staff, who tirelessly deciphered my handwriting to type the manuscript—only to proofread, edit, and revise it. I also want to thank my editor, Debra Petrosky, who encouraged and counseled me in bringing the book to fruition.

PREFACE

This is not a New Age book!

It has nothing to do with the occult.

This book is in no way associated with psychology.

Many people see a book on this subject and automatically assume it fits one of the above categories. That's understandable. New Agers, occult devotees, and psychologists have delved into the area of dreams—and they're not shy about sharing their beliefs.

This book is written to help Bible-believing Christians hear from God in the night season—a very scriptural experience. Allow me to escort you on an introductory tour into a world that has often been misunderstood and misrepresented, a place whose terrain has been mapped in Scripture—the God-given world of dreams.

INTRODUCTION

When I was a very young Christian, I attended a church service where a woman testified that God had spoken to her in a dream. What? My ears perked up. Did I hear her right? Does God really speak to people in dreams? As soon as I got home that night, I knelt beside my bed and talked to God.

"Lord," I asked, "is it really true that You talk to people in dreams? If so, please talk to me in a dream tonight."

That simple prayer launched me on an exciting adventure in hearing from God. Upon waking up the next morning, I recalled a very vivid, significant dream. Enthusiasm about hearing from God in this way flooded me. I could hardly wait to explore this new frontier! And explore it I did!

From that time on, God began to teach me how to receive and interpret dreams. Since I knew no Christians who had experience in this field, I slowly and painstakingly walked through the learning process myself. Over a period of years, God taught me many truths about this relevant means of communication.

Step by step, experience by experience, scripture by scripture, He gradually built my knowledge in this field. Patterns began to emerge. Principles began to form. Pieces began to fit together. By carefully recording and analyzing my dreams, I gleaned knowledge, wisdom, and skill in hearing from God in the night season. Proof after convincing proof assured me that God was speaking to me and that He will speak to you through dreams—continually and regularly.

It's really true!

You're about to benefit from wisdom that took me years to accumulate. I'll do my best to lead you step by step through the different facets of this exciting frontier. As your tour guide in the world of dreams, I'll be as thorough and comprehensive as possible. We'll move carefully so you receive a complete, detailed orientation. Join me as we explore the world that Daniel and Joseph obviously pioneered centuries ago—the world of dreams.

1

THE WORLD OF DREAMS

Welcome to a world within our world! This world is fresh, new, and exciting because it's part of the prophetic move of God in our generation. This world is also as old as recorded history. Job, the oldest book in the Bible, reveals some of its territory. Its challenging terrain is as old as events written in Genesis and as new as events prophesied in the book of Revelation.

This virgin world is virtually unexplored, yet it bears the signs of having been walked through many times in history. Some pioneers have examined it carefully during regular expeditions; others have captured only glimpses of it during brief encounters.

Superstitions and rumors abound about the inner recesses of this world. Thinking this world is a place of immense danger, many have shied away from crossing its borders. Some think demons control this world. Still others have dismissed it as a place where only fantasies and products of vivid, wild imaginations occupy its territories.

You may sense some apprehension about venturing across the threshold into this unfamiliar world. You may have been warned against it! Perhaps for a good reason, too!

Normal, intelligent people don't just plunge head first into unknown waters. Yet I have three questions for you:

1. Do you want to hear God's voice with clarity?

2. Do you want to walk in the fullness of God's Spirit?

3. Do you want to be on the cutting edge of all that God is doing in the end times?

Listen, friend. Don't throw caution to the wind because of your desire to grow in God. Consider the apostle Paul's wise counsel about evaluating doctrine. *"Test all things; hold fast what is good"* (1 Thessalonians 5:21).

Don't you agree? Why not heed this counsel while hearing my story? God led me to venture into this world I've been describing. He directed me to enter it again and again. He commissioned me to explore it carefully, cautiously, and thoroughly. He spent—and I invested—years developing my knowledge of its inner terrain, its content, and its territories. As an experienced guide, I'm qualified to lead you on an exploratory trip into its innermost realm.

Before you join me, however, why not read what I've learned about making such a trip? You don't have to jump into this before considering the benefits and risks of such a journey. After taking this exploratory trip, you can make your own judgments about entering this world. At least, you'll act on a well thought out decision, not a spur-of-the-moment whim. I'm sure you realize that the world I've been describing is the world of dreams.

You Can Receive Dreams from God

Does God speak to people in dreams? Will He speak to *you* in *your* dreams? If so, how can you tell when God speaks to you through a dream and when He doesn't? If God gives you a dream, how will you know the interpretation?

Christians have many questions about this intriguing subject, but they've found little teaching available to answer their questions.

Using the foundation of Scripture and personal experience, this book will answer many of your questions concerning dreams.

Man has been dreaming since his creation. Throughout history, God has used dreams to communicate to men. The numerous dreams in the Bible confirm that this is a valid channel through which God speaks to His people. This unusual avenue of receiving God-inspired direction is just beginning to come into its prime. God is accelerating the use of this communication vehicle in an unprecedented manner as we enter the end times!

Dreams will play a vital role in imparting God's guidance to His people in the coming days. In these last days, we shall "dream dreams." (See Joel 2:28; Acts 2:17.)

God is a God of many voices. Let's look at Scripture to find out how God communicates to men.

> God, who **at various times** and **in different ways** spoke in time past to the fathers by the prophets, has in these last days spoken to us by His Son.(Hebrews 1:1–2, emphasis added)

God speaks in many ways. He wants His people to be skillful in hearing Him in all of the ways that He speaks. Dreams are one form of communication between God and man. In fact, dreams will be one of the common ways through which He will speak to believers in days to come.

Please consider the following statement with an open mind. Remember the apostle Paul's encouragement to *"test all things; hold fast what is good"* (1 Thessalonians 5:21). I challenge you to heed this scriptural admonition as you consider this statement:

> You can learn to receive dreams from God. You can receive them regularly, and you can develop skill in interpreting dreams. Dreams and their interpretations can become a key method of receiving direction from God in all your affairs.

This book presents a solid, scriptural basis from which you can develop this ability in your own life. The principles you're about to read can be invaluable to you as God begins to speak to you through dreams. These teachings have sparked dramatic, life-changing experiences for countless others, and they can do the same for you.

Come with me and let's explore the fascinating world of dreams. After showing you where this territory is mapped in Scripture, I'll add my personal experience and insight to help you travel in this land.

What Are Dreams?

Dreams are a series of thoughts, images, or emotions that occur during sleep. I haven't ever met a person who did not remember having a dream of some kind during his lifetime. Daniel called dreams *"visions of his head upon his bed"* (Daniel 7:1, KJV).

The Bible generally teaches truth through a direct statement or through a demonstration, example, or pattern. Dreams are presented in the Bible in both of these ways as a valid means for God to communicate to man. Let's look at two direct statements about dreams.

> *In a dream, in a vision of the night, when deep sleep falls upon men, while slumbering on their beds, then [God] opens the ears of men, and seals their instruction.* (Job 33:15–16)

> *And it shall come to pass in the last days, says God, that I will pour out of My Spirit on all flesh; your sons and your daughters shall prophesy, your young men shall see visions, your old men shall dream dreams.* (Acts 2:17)

The Bible also demonstrates that God talked to men in this manner throughout history. In fact, God does not limit Himself to speaking to just His people in dreams. Remember the scheme that Abram pulled?

> *And it came to pass, when [Abram] was close to entering Egypt, that he said to Sarai his wife, "Indeed I know that you are a woman of beautiful countenance. Therefore it will happen, when the Egyptians see you, that they will say, 'This is his wife'; and they will kill me, but they will let you live. Please say you are my sister, that it may be well with me for your sake, and that I may live because of you."* (Genesis 12:11–13)

Pharaoh took Sarai into his household and was struck with plagues. Recognizing God's judgment, he sent the couple away. A few chapters later, however, Abraham relied on the same trickery. This time Abimelech, king of Gerar, took Abraham's "sister" into his household. What did God do?

> *But God came to Abimelech **in a dream by night**, and said to him, "Indeed you are a dead man because of the woman whom you have taken, for she is a man's wife." But Abimelech had not come near her; and he said, "Lord, will You slay a righteous nation also? Did he not say to me, 'She is my sister'? And she, even she herself said, 'He is my brother.' In the integrity of my heart and innocence of my hands I have done this." And God said to him **in a dream**, "Yes, I know that you did this in the integrity of your heart. For I also withheld you from sinning against Me; therefore I did not let you touch her."*
> (Genesis 20:3–6, emphasis added)

Starting with this example, God establishes dreams as a scriptural way for Him to communicate to men. God used dreams to speak to people in the Old and New Testaments, including Joseph, Pharaoh, Jacob, Solomon, Nebuchadnezzar, Daniel, and others.

Saved from Starvation

God also preserved His people during a severe famine by using Joseph to interpret a dream given to Pharaoh, the Egyptian ruler. The Hebrew youth, sold into slavery by his brothers, was unjustly accused by Potiphar's wife and imprisoned. Even in the dungeon, however, Joseph distinguished himself by his conduct and ability to interpret dreams.

Angered with his chief butler and chief baker, Pharaoh imprisoned them with Joseph. The two officers had dreams on the same night and were saddened at not understanding them. Joseph listened to the dreams, gave the interpretations, and requested that the butler remember him when Pharaoh restored him to his position. Two years later, when Pharaoh had a puzzling dream that no one could interpret, the butler finally remembered Joseph's amazing ability.

Then Pharaoh sent and called Joseph, and they brought him hastily out of the dungeon; and he shaved, changed his clothing, and came to Pharaoh. And Pharaoh said to Joseph, "I have dreamed a dream, and there is no one who can interpret it. But I have heard it said of you that you can understand a dream, to interpret it." So Joseph answered Pharaoh, saying, "It is not in me; God will give Pharaoh an answer of peace." Then Pharaoh said to Joseph: "Behold, in my dream I stood on the bank of the river. Suddenly seven cows came up out of the river, fine looking and fat; and they fed in the meadow. Then behold, seven other cows came up after them, poor and very ugly and gaunt, such ugliness as I have never seen in all the land of Egypt. And the gaunt and ugly cows ate up the first seven, the fat cows. When they had eaten them up, no one would have known that they had eaten them, for they were just as ugly as at the beginning. So I awoke. Also I saw in my dream, and suddenly seven heads came up on one stalk, full and good. Then behold, seven heads, withered, thin, and blighted by the east wind, sprang up after them. And the thin heads devoured the seven good heads. So I told this to the magicians, but there was no one who could explain it to me." Then Joseph said to Pharaoh, "The dreams of Pharaoh are one: God has shown Pharaoh what He is about to do: The seven good cows are seven years, and the seven good heads are seven years; the dreams are one. And the seven thin and ugly cows which came up after them are seven years, and the seven empty heads blighted by the east wind are seven years of famine....."Indeed seven years of great plenty will come throughout all the land of Egypt; but after them seven years of famine will arise, and all the plenty will be forgotten in the land of Egypt; and the famine will deplete the land. So the plenty will not be known in the land because of the famine following, for it will be very severe. And the dream was repeated to Pharaoh twice because the thing is established by God, and God will shortly bring it to pass." (Genesis 41:14–32)

God used a dream to warn Pharaoh about an upcoming famine. Pharaoh heeded the warning and set Joseph over the land as an administrator. The famine affected the whole world, but Egypt had planned ahead for the crisis. They even sold grain to other nations, which resulted in saving Joseph's family from starvation.

Confidence in Battle

Despite conquering the king of Canaan and enjoying forty years of rest, Israel sinned and incurred God's judgment. The Midianites destroyed their land, plundered their livestock, and terrorized the people.

While Gideon timidly threshed wheat in his father's wine-press, an angel appeared to him. "The Lord is with you, you mighty man of valor!" he greeted him. *"Go in this might of yours, and you shall save Israel from the hand of the Midianites. Have I not sent you?"* (Judges 6:14).

This reluctant deliverer asked, *"O my* LORD, *how can I save Israel? Indeed my clan is the weakest in Manasseh, and I am the least in my father's house"* (Judges 6:15). Gideon needed confirmation that God would use him to deliver Israel. Several miraculous signs from God bolstered Gideon's confidence.

Approximately 32,000 Israelites rallied behind Gideon, but God pared down his fighting forces to three hundred men. His small band carried pitchers, torches, and trumpets against a vast army. Knowing Gideon's apprehension, God gave him the following instructions:

Arise, go down against the camp, for I have delivered it into your hand. But if you are afraid to go down, go down to the camp with Purah your servant, and you shall hear what they say; and afterward your hands shall be strengthened to go down against the camp. (Judges 7:9–11)

Gideon and his servant traveled to the outpost of the enemy camp where he heard a conversation that injected him with courage.

And when Gideon had come, there was a man telling a dream to his companion. He said, "I have just had a dream: To my surprise, a loaf of barley bread tumbled into the camp of Midian; it came to a tent and struck it so that it fell and over-turned, and the tent collapsed." Then his companion answered and said, "This is nothing else but the sword of Gideon the son of Joash, a man of Israel; for into his hand God has delivered

Midian and the whole camp." And so it was, when Gideon heard the telling of the dream and its interpretation, that he worshiped. He returned to the camp of Israel, and said, "Arise, for the LORD has delivered the camp of Midian into your hand."   (Judges 7:13–15)

Upon hearing the dream and its interpretation, Gideon obtained the confidence he needed to conquer the Midianites. Knowing that he had heard from God, Gideon led three hundred men against a vast army and defeated them.

Warning and Direction

God also uses dreams to give guidance, direction, and warning. Those who obeyed these timely messages from God averted misunderstanding, mishaps, and even death. Let's look at a few examples.

Joseph, who was betrothed to Mary, discovered some disconcerting news from his bride-to-be. Before they were married, Mary had conceived a child. Being a just man, Joseph didn't want to humiliate her publicly. As he considered putting her away secretly, he received specific instructions in a dream.

*But while he thought about these things, behold, an angel of the Lord appeared to him **in a dream**, saying, "Joseph, son of David, do not be afraid to take to you Mary your wife, for that which is conceived in her is of the Holy Spirit. And she will bring forth a Son, and you shall call His name Jesus, for He will save His people from their sins."*

(Matthew 1:20–21, emphasis added)

After the birth of Christ, wise men from the east came to worship the newborn King. Herod was also interested in discovering the location of this prophesied ruler. His motive, however, was to eliminate his competition for the throne.

> *Now after Jesus was born in Bethlehem of Judea in the days of Herod the king, behold, wise men from the East came to Jerusalem, saying, "Where is He who has been born King of the Jews? For we have seen His star in the East and have come to worship Him." When Herod the king heard these things, he was troubled, and all Jerusalem with him....Then Herod, when he had secretly called the wise men, determined from them what time the star appeared. And he sent them to Bethlehem and said, "Go and search diligently for the young Child; and when you have found Him, bring back word to me, that I may come and worship Him also."*
>
> (Matthew 2:1–3, 7–8)

The star that the wise men had followed from the East also led them to Jesus. After worshiping and presenting their gifts, did they inform Herod of His whereabouts? No!

> *Then, being divinely warned in a dream that they should not return to Herod, they departed for their own country another way. Now when they had departed, behold, an angel of the Lord appeared to Joseph **in a dream**, saying, "Arise, take the young Child and His mother, flee to Egypt, and stay there until I bring you word; for Herod will seek the young Child to destroy Him."*   (Matthew 2:12–13, emphasis added)

When he arose, Joseph took his family by night and traveled to Egypt. Angered that the wise men had deceived him by not returning, Herod commissioned soldiers to slay all the male children in Bethlehem who were two years old and younger. Jesus escaped certain death because of Joseph's obedience to his dream. God also used a dream to tell Joseph when to return to Israel.

> *But when Herod was dead, behold, an angel of the Lord
> appeared **in a dream** to Joseph in Egypt, saying, "Arise, take
> the young Child and His mother, and go to the land of Israel,
> for those who sought the young Child's life are dead." Then
> he arose, took the young Child and His mother, and came
> into the land of Israel. But when he heard that Archelaus was
> reigning over Judea instead of his father Herod, he was afraid
> to go there. And being warned by God **in a dream**, he turned
> aside into the region of Galilee. And he came and dwelt in a
> city called Nazareth.* (Matthew 2:19–23, emphasis added)

Joseph received divine guidance in his dreams on several
occasions. God led him at key points by communicating His will
during the night seasons.

Are Dreams Valid Today?

These Bible passages prove that dreams have played a significant role in our Christian heritage. But what about the times in
which we live? Christians are living in what many believe is the
last generation before the return of Christ. Are dreams relevant
to us today? Dear Christian friend, the answer is unequivocally
"Yes!" Dreams are more pertinent today than they have been since
the beginning of history. God wants to speak to you in a variety of
ways. Dreams are certainly one of those ways.

God revealed His nature when He said, *"For I am the Lord,
I do not change"* (Malachi 3:6). God created man and gave him
the ability to dream. God has demonstrated His use of dreams
as a way to speak to man throughout the Bible. Has He suddenly
changed so that He no longer does this?

No, of course not! God still speaks to men in dreams. Receiving
dreams is an indication that the Holy Spirit has been poured out
in these last days!

And it shall come to pass in the last days, says God, that I will pour out of My Spirit on all flesh; your sons and your daughters shall prophesy, your young men shall see visions, your old men shall dream dreams.   (Acts 2:17)

Do you see it?

Dreams are scriptural!

Dreams are for today!

And dreams are for you!

God is raising up a church that will move in signs and wonders. He wants His people to be knowledgeable in the ways of the Holy Spirit. God is raising up Josephs and Daniels who will understand the language of the Holy Spirit, including receiving and interpreting dreams.

Spared through a Dream

While teaching a seminar on how to hear the voice of God, I covered a section on dreams. Most dreams need to be interpreted, but sometimes a message spoken by a character in a dream can be literal. Soon after I left town, a woman who had attended the seminar experienced a dream in which her pastor gave her a scripture. After she awakened, she opened her Bible and looked up the verse. The scripture referred to bearing children.

How could this be? Her doctor had told her she could have no more children.

That very day doctors diagnosed her daughter as having parasites in her digestive tract. This contagious condition often spread to other family members. The doctor gave the entire family a prescription to eradicate the parasites from their systems. Just as the woman was about to take the medication, she noticed a warning on the container: *Warning. Not to be taken if pregnant. Medication could result in death or miscarriage of unborn child. If you suspect pregnancy, please consult a physician.*

The woman had no reason to suspect pregnancy. As a matter of fact, she had been assured by physicians that she could not get pregnant. But she remembered her dream. Just to be safe, she abstained from taking the medicine and took a pregnancy test. Amazingly, she tested positive! The next time I traveled through that area, she showed me her miracle baby. Jesus was not the only baby whose life was saved through a dream!

Striking a Winning Blow

A young pastor came to me for help. He had heard that God often gave me interpretations of dreams. This man and his family had experienced some rough times as they sought God's direction during a period of transition.

The pastor had dreamed he was fighting a man in a boxing ring. After sparring with his opponent for a few rounds, he drew back his fist and landed a knockout blow, ending the fight. As he related the dream, I questioned him about different parts of it.

"Did you know the man you were fighting?" I asked. "Who was he?"

"Oh, he was just a man I used to know a long time ago," he said. "I haven't seen him in years."

"Who was the man?" I pressed him for a more specific answer. "What was his relationship with you in the past?"

"To tell you the truth, this man used to buy beer for my friends and me when we were in high school. I wasn't living for the Lord then, and we were too young to buy beer. This man used to buy it for us."

"Have you been having a battle with alcohol?" I asked.

Suddenly, he broke and began to weep. "I never thought it could happen to me, but it did. When everything was at its lowest, a friend and I drank some beer, and now I can't seem to stop. I'm scared!" he confided.

"Brother," I told him, "keep fighting. You're going to conquer that sin and get the victory!"

"Do you really think so?" he asked.

"Yes, I'm sure of it." As I told him that, his countenance changed as hope entered his spirit. I prayed for him then, and he left with a new faith and determination to win his battle against alcohol. He did just that, too. He's been back in the ministry for many years with no recurrence of that problem!

These examples of people receiving help through dreams are only two out of hundreds that I know from personal experience. Dreams can be a powerful means through which God gives guidance, hope, and victory to His people.

What about the Occult?

As I explored the world of dreams, I found a small section of land that contained some strange-looking inhabitants. They were poor, sickly, miserable-looking creatures.

"Who are these people?" I asked the Lord.

"Those are members of the occult. They think this land belongs to them, but they're wrong! That's the reason they're not flourishing here."

Don't let occultists put their fence around our God-given territory, bluffing us with their "keep off" signs. We're the rightful owners of this land in the first place.

Today people often seek astrologers and fortune-tellers to understand their dreams. This is nothing new. King Nebuchadnezzar grew troubled over dreams that he didn't understand, so he sought the astrologers. But the king challenged his court magicians with a more difficult request.

The king said to them, "I have had a dream, and my spirit is anxious to know the dream." Then the Chaldeans spoke to the king in Aramaic, "O king, live forever! Tell your servants the dream, and we will give the interpretation." But the king answered and said to the Chaldeans, "My decision is firm: if you do not make known the dream to me, and its interpretation, you shall be cut in pieces, and your houses shall be made an ash heap. However, if you tell the dream and its interpretation, you shall receive from me gifts, rewards, and great honor. Therefore tell me the dream and its interpretation." (Daniel 2:3–6)

Nebuchadnezzar discovered that his magicians, astrologers, and soothsayers couldn't give the dream and its interpretation when they were challenged—even though their lives depended on it. As Daniel sought the Lord, the secret was revealed to him in a night vision. (See Daniel 2 :4–19.)

Today people repeat Nebuchadnezzar's mistake by consulting psychologists or those who delve into the occult to understand their dreams. But the occultists couldn't produce results in Nebuchadnezzar's day, and they'll miss the mark in our day, too. For the sake of this scriptural study, let's forget modern terms such as "psychology" and "subconscious mind" and approach the subject of dreams as a simple, scriptural, and practical way for God to give you direction and guidance in your daily life.

As I explored the vast regions of this new territory, I occasionally found a few straggling, confused people who always seemed to be in pairs or small groups.

"Who are they?" I asked the Lord.

"Those are the fruits, flakes, and nuts," God told me. "They've fallen into error by chasing some dream they didn't understand. They've gotten into a mess by ignoring common sense and scriptural warnings. They're giving the place a bad name."

We must not let the fruits, flakes, and nuts intimidate us into withdrawing from our God-given territory. I even know some flakes who have fallen into error by misinterpreting verses of Scripture. Does that keep me from reading the Bible? No! On the contrary, it should cause me to study the Bible even more to ground myself in its truth.

Let's grow up and launch out in the things of the Spirit that are freely given to us by God. You can safely develop your ability to hear from God without wandering into left field with the fruits, flakes, and nuts. That's exactly what I'll show you in this book.

Ask God to Prove It!

Don't let prejudices, preconceived ideas, or unscriptural views cause you to limit God as He reveals Himself in dreams in these last days. Consider what I'm teaching and ask God to prove it to you. I believe He will do just that!

While teaching a seminar at a church in northern Alabama, I mentioned dreams. God often wakes a person at the end of a dream to enable him to pull the dream out of his memory while it's still fresh. The pastor of the church decided to test my teaching, so he prayed before he went to bed that night. He had been perplexed by a situation and wanted God's guidance. Perhaps God would visit him in the night season and give him the solution he had been seeking.

Sure enough, he awakened from his sleep in the early morning hours. Following my instructions, he immediately searched his memory. A dream, which otherwise might have been lost, drifted into his memory. As he reflected on it, the dream gave him the answer he had been seeking! Nevertheless, he asked God to confirm the answer in the Word. He went to the den, got his Bible, and promptly opened it up. God spoke to him through Scripture that morning and confirmed the answer.

Yes, God can prove things to us in such a way that we know we're hearing from Him. If you've followed the Lord for any time at all, you know this is true. When hearing from God in an unfamiliar area like dreams, He would expect you to seek His confirmations. God will give convincing proofs that He is speaking to you in the night season.

Let's continue our exploratory journey to find out more about hearing from God in dreams.

We'll proceed slowly, cautiously, and safely.

Let's be careful.

There's no hurry.

There's no need to jump to any conclusions until we've covered more ground, is there?

Shall we look into this world a little further? I would like to begin by telling you about several of my early visits to it as a young Christian.

Come along.

2

AN INVALUABLE
SOURCE OF GUIDANCE

Soon after becoming a Christian, I formed a gospel trio. We traveled and sang at churches within a four or five hour drive of our hometown. Our trio desperately needed a van in which to travel and to carry our sound equipment. A series of events raised our hopes of getting a van—and taught me invaluable truths about dream interpretation. Here's how it happened.

One Saturday morning we sang at the Houston Full Gospel Businessmen's monthly meeting. After the meeting, while I was loading the sound equipment, I noticed that the two women who were in the trio with me were praying with a well-known evangelist. A few moments later, they ran to me and bubbled over with excitement.

"Guess what?" they asked. "We just asked her to pray with us about a van to travel in! She prayed, 'Lord, give this group a van, give it to them by June 1, and let it be paid for.'"

Wow! Her specific prayer thrilled us! That petition set off an amazing chain of events. Only two weeks later, we were ministering in a church. After the meeting, a group of us were praying and waiting before the Lord. The guest minister for the evening suddenly spoke.

"The Lord just gave me a vision," he declared. "I saw a white van for this singing group—and it was all paid for. I believe God is going to give you a van to travel in!" If we were excited before, we were really excited now! Both incidents predicted that the van would be paid for. Hallelujah!

The next clue heightened my curiosity even more. A few days later, I ran an errand for my wife. She needed something from our local shopping mall. After picking up her purchase, I headed toward my car. In mid-stride, however, a familiar prompting in my spirit stopped me. "Go into the main mall area," the Holy Spirit nudged. As a young Christian, I had often received God's guidance by following these promptings. I turned and walked to the main mall. As soon as I got inside, I looked around, trying to figure out why God sent me there.

Then I saw them—vans! Everywhere! That particular day was van display day. Plush, customized vans filled the walkways. How exciting! I looked and looked. Surely God had a van for our group somewhere! As I admired the different models, I could just see our trio traveling together in a van!

My excitement and anticipation grew every day. June 1 was getting closer and closer. Then came the dreams.

In the first dream, I was driving my car. I pulled off the road, got out of the car, and walked toward a nearby motel. I noticed that the scenery by the road appeared in sections. The first section was a field. The next section was trees. Then I saw a pond. The final section was a fence and some blue sky.

As I approached the motel, I noticed my banker's car in the parking lot. Convinced that it was his car, I approached the check-in desk in the lobby and asked for him.

"I'm sorry, sir, but there's no one here by that name," the desk clerk apologized.

"But I'm sure that was his car," I replied.

"I'm sorry, sir, but no one by that name is on my register."

I turned away in confusion. I was *sure*   that was his car. Just then another employee from my bank walked past me. "Dave!" I called out. I reached up and put my hand on his shoulder. He whirled to look at me, but it wasn't Dave! Twice I thought people from my bank were at this motel, but they weren't! As I returned to my car, I noticed the scenery in sections. I saw the fence, the blue sky, and the field. But wait! A piece of the scenery—the pond—was missing. What had happened to it?

Then, I woke up.

Needless to say, I didn't understand the dream. I simply recorded it in the composition book that I keep by my bedside and dated it. Perhaps I would understand it later.

A few nights later, I had another dream. In this dream, I was shopping for a van in a used car lot. The dealer had a white van that looked good. I opened the door and looked at the odometer. All the digits on the odometer lined up perfectly. Yet, in the dream, I felt I was not supposed to buy this van. Again, I woke up, wrote the dream down, and pondered the meaning.

"This Must Be the Van!"

While these events were taking place, June first was rapidly approaching. If God was about to provide a van for us, He had better do it soon! Of course, I also knew that "*faith by itself, if it does not have works, is dead*" (James 2:17).

With only a week to go before the deadline, I woke up early on a Saturday morning to look for a van. After praying, I felt impressed to drive down Eleventh Street. After driving a short distance, I paused at a red light. As I waited for the light to change, I spotted a white van with a "For Sale" sign in the window! The owner had parked it in front of a well known Christian businessman's place of business! Wow! I was excited!

I turned into the parking lot of the business, got out of my car, and walked toward the van. As I got closer, I noticed the sign of a fish painted on the side. "Glory Express" was printed in beautiful, large letters below the Christian emblem. It really looked sharp!

As I looked through the window, I spotted an eight-track tape player with a gospel tape in it. This had to be the van that all those clues led me to! I found it only a week before the June 1 deadline! I went inside, found the owner— someone I already knew—and asked him about the van.

"We've been trying to sell that van for several months. You know, it's the strangest thing. No one seems to be interested in it," he informed me. "I've never driven the van to work before. But for some reason, this morning I decided to drive the van instead of my car. When I got here, I was going to park it in the back, but at the last minute I decided to park it in front. You drove up only five minutes later."

Wow! All the pieces fit! This must be the van God had chosen for me. Then he added something that clinched it for me. He said, "You know, that van used to belong to an evangelist. We bought it to carry neighborhood kids to Sunday school. We've been praying that God would keep it in His work somehow."

Now I was convinced! "Brother," I told him, "I'm sure this is the van God has picked out for me!"

"Why don't you take it home and let your wife look at it while I talk to my wife about the asking price?"

"Great!" I responded.

I started up the van, turned on the tape player, and drove it home. It was perfect! My wife and kids loved it! Then, on the way back to the man's business, I decided to stop by my church. After locating one of the elders, I explained the amazing chain of events that led me to this van. He and I laid hands on the van and claimed it for the ministry.

When I returned the van, I said, "Brother, I think the Lord wants me to have that van. How much are you asking?"

"We were asking $4,000," he replied, "but since it's for the Lord's work, we have decided to ask $3,000. That's what we're actually carrying it for on our books."

My mind quickly began to race! There was only one week left until June 1. "I would like you to do me a favor," I ventured. "Can you hold the van for me for one week? I believe things will work out for me to have the money by then."

"No problem. We've had no bites on the van in four months. I see no problem in waiting another week."

Excitement pumped through my veins! What a testimony this would be! God had a week to come up with my miracle! I didn't even consider financing the van because of the words that indicated it would be completely paid for! I expectantly waited for the money to come in.

How would the money come? Perhaps it would come in the mail! Maybe God would even prompt the Christian businessman to give it to us! However God decided to provide, it would be great!

My Faith Suffers a Setback

Every day of the following week I called the businessman to see if there was any change. Each time I asked, "Anything new on the van, brother? God hasn't sent the money yet, but I still believe He's going to."

On Wednesday, only three days before June first, I called to check on the van.

"Any new developments?" I asked.

"Brother, I've got some bad news about the van."

"What do you mean?"

"We sold the van."

"*You what?*"

"We sold it," he repeated.

"But I don't understand. You said you would hold it for me!" I was shocked! I *knew* I had heard from God! The pieces all fit. How could this be?

"Someone offered us $4,000 for the van. We prayed and really felt we were to sell it."

I couldn't believe it!

"The deal will fall through," I offered.

"I don't think so," he replied. "These people really seem to want it."

"Well, I'll check back on it tomorrow."

After hanging up, I got more concerned. What was going on? Disappointment had pierced my faith. God will make a way, I told myself. Knowing I must be strong, I set my faith to not waver.

The next day I called again. "What happened? Did the people change their minds?"

"No, brother. They came in, we signed the papers, and they drove off in the van."

"The check's going to bounce," I lamely responded.

"They paid for it with a cashier's check."

"They'll change their mind."

"I don't think so. They seemed to be very pleased with the van."

"Well, if something does come up, please call me," I said, finishing our conversation.

My head was reeling! How could it be? I was so sure I had heard from God! I left work early and went home very discouraged and dejected.

When I got home, the full brunt of it hit me! Not getting the van had damaged my faith. I cried out to God from the depths of my emotions. He had hurt me! I had trusted Him, and He had let me down!

"God, You set me up to get hurt. All the pieces lined up. Why did You let this happen?" Then I told God what was really in my heart. "I will serve You, but I can't guarantee that I will ever trust You again."

Missing God

Now what was I going to do? I decided to drive to the Christian bookstore. Maybe I could find a book that would help me. When I walked into the bookstore, I glanced at hundreds of books that lined the shelves. As I strolled down an aisle, I began to pray. Not knowing which book to get, I tried be sensitive to the promptings of the Holy Spirit. I felt impressed to pick up a certain book. Thinking it might help me, I decided to buy it. Then I spied a book that I had already read. I remembered that it had really bolstered my faith. Maybe I should buy it, too. Needing all the encouragement I could get, I purchased both books.

When I got home, I quickly settled into my favorite chair and began to read the first book. The more I read, the more I realized it didn't relate at all to what I was going through. Frustrated by my choice, I put it down. I picked up the book that I had bought at the last minute.

Then it happened! I immediately opened the book to the author's description of a time when he missed God. He *thought* the pieces had lined up, but he was mistaken. I had opened the book at random and began to read at that very spot! How does God do that? It happens to me often and never ceases to amaze me!

As I read the author's account of how he thought the pieces lined up, I wondered, Could this have happened to me? I considered all the indications of God's leading and how they seemed to fit together so perfectly.

Then, I remembered the dreams! I ran to the bedroom to retrieve my dream book. I thumbed through my recent written accounts of dreams, searching for one that would fit. I found my first dream that related to the van. As I read it, my heart began to leap. It fit! I thought my banker was there, but he wasn't! As I walked from the motel, I noticed that one piece of the scenery was missing! My thoughts began to race. The banker stood for finances. The finances were missing! No wonder the money hadn't come in. God had warned me through the dream!

Then, I found my second dream. I was looking at a used white van. Although all the digits on the odometer lined up, I was not supposed to buy the van. It also fit perfectly! All the pieces *seemed* to line up, but I wasn't supposed to buy the van. God had not misled me after all! As a matter of fact, *the dreams were the safety factors that God gave to keep me from being misled!*

Don't you see the importance of hearing from God in dreams? A dream can be the very means by which God can speak to you to keep you on the right track—even when you may be missing Him in other ways! Hearing from God in a variety of ways provides a safety net for believers.

A man once told me, "Following dreams can get you off track." I've got news for him. There's another side to that coin! Dreams are the very method that God often uses to keep me *on* track.

Bargaining for a Van

Only a few weeks later (June 1 had already passed), my wife Sandy found a classified ad for a used van that looked interesting. She called me at work and suggested I look at it.

"Good idea," I told her. "I'll drive by and look at it after lunch." I called the number listed in the ad and asked for directions. The house was outside the city limits and the directions were fairly complex, so I carefully wrote them down. I went home to eat lunch that day and then left to look at the van. Suddenly I realized that I had left the directions on my desk. "Oh, well," I said, "I'll try to remember them. If God is in it, maybe I'll find the house anyway." To my surprise, the directions came back to me, and I drove right up to the house out in the country.

The van sat in front of the house. It was white, and it looked good. The woman told me they were asking $2,900 for the van. "Why don't you have your husband call me this evening when he gets off work?" I suggested. "I'm interested in the van." She wrote down my phone number and agreed to have him call.

Driving back to the office, I recalled all the events concerning vans that had transpired in the past few months. Suddenly, my thoughts were interrupted by some words. The words came in the form of a thought—not an audible voice—but they did not emanate from my mind. My mind was actually thinking about something else when the words came up from my spirit. The words were simply: "Twenty six hundred."

As I pondered this, I realized that the Lord apparently wanted me to pay no more than $2,600 for the van. This was foreign to my thinking because I thought $2,900 was a fair price. Nevertheless, I decided to offer the man $2,600 when he called.

That evening, the owner of the van called around six o'clock. After briefly discussing his vehicle, I asked him if he would consider taking less than $2,900.

"No," he replied, "we believe we're asking the right price at $2,900."

"Why don't you talk it over with your wife and call me back?" I suggested. "I'm willing to make a firm offer of $ 2,600, no more."

"I'll talk to her," he said, "but I'm sure we won't go down on the price."

Thirty minutes later my phone rang again. "Mr. Thomas, we discussed the price on the van. Like I told you, we feel that our price is fair. My wife agrees that we shouldn't lower the price." Then the man spent five minutes telling me why the van was worth $2,900. After closing his convincing argument, he completely surprised me by saying, "But I'm inclined to go ahead and let you have it for $2,600."

Convinced this was the vehicle God wanted us to have, I bought the van. Our singing group finally had a spacious vehicle in which to travel. How did we pay for it? I took out a ninety day renewable note at the bank. We paid off the note during the next eighteen months. God faithfully supplied the money over a period of time.

A very interesting sequel to this story highlights God's wisdom. Shortly after purchasing the van, I noticed a wobble in the wheels. "The brakes are completely gone in this van," the mechanic reported. "It looks like someone intentionally loosened the wheels to conceal the noise you would hear from the brakes rubbing together. Driving around this way is dangerous."

How much did it cost to get the brakes repaired? Exactly $300—the difference between $2,900 and $2,600. Did God look out for us or what? Throughout this entire progression of events, we got our van. And during the process I learned a lot about God's nature and how to hear from Him.

Are You a Seeker?

Why does God speak in a variety of ways—and why did He choose dreams as one of them? One of the reasons involves the nature of God. Scripture says, *"He who comes to God must believe that He is, and that He is a rewarder of those who diligently seek Him"* (Hebrews 11:6).

God likes a seeker. He encourages us to seek Him and His ways. Jesus told His disciples, *"Ask, and it will be given to you; seek, and you will find; knock, and it will be opened to you"* (Matthew 7:7). Another verse highlights this point. Solomon wrote, *"It is the glory of God to conceal a matter, but the glory of kings is to search out a matter"* (Proverbs 25:2, emphasis added). God conceals or hides truths, and He likes for us to find them.

Since God speaks in a variety of ways—and we don't know which way He may communicate next—we must be watching, listening, and seeking Him in all the ways that He speaks. When I have this attitude, I always stay close to God.

God wants you to be alert to all the ways He communicates. Seek Him in the morning in the Scriptures. Watch for Him in the circumstances that you encounter during the day. Listen for Him during your prayer time. You can even learn to watch for Him in the night season. If you do this, you'll be pleasing Him. You'll also be hearing from Him—no matter how He chooses to speak!

When my two daughters were growing up, we often visited their grandfather and grandmother at their camp on the nearby

Sabine River. Grandma often bought a toy for the girls and hid it. Then she wrote clues on several pieces of paper. Each clue led to the next clue, until the girls finally found the prize. When we arrived at the camp, Grandma greeted us and often said, "Girls, go look under the swing." The girls giggled and raced to the swing. There they searched until they found the first piece of paper. Then they unfolded it and read the next clue. Finally, after finding and reading each clue, they found the prize.

A good detective constantly sifts and sorts clues, trying to make them fit together. His goal is to solve the mystery. But he must use all the available facts toe arrive at the right conclusions.

Following God is the same way. He often speaks in pieces, and each piece fits together to convey His full message. Dreams complement the other ways that God speaks. Your dreams may hold the key to some important guidance. As you learn to hear from God in dreams, add this information to the other clues that God gives you. God's message will become increasingly clear to you.

Bypassing the Minds

Dreams can be an invaluable source of guidance. People who aren't accustomed to hearing from God in dreams may not realize this fact. Occasionally someone asks me, "I already hear from God in other ways. Why do I need to hear from Him in dreams?"

When you dream, your conscious mind is asleep. During the night season God can bypass your logic, your preconceived notions, and the other obstacles of your conscious mind. God can use dreams to get through to you when other avenues may fail. Has God ever tried to show you something, but you weren't hearing Him? Have you ever misunderstood His use of circumstances, Scripture, or the promptings of the Holy Spirit? That's why you need to be able to hear from God in dreams.

Another important reason for hearing from God in a variety of ways—including dreams—is safety. When you're hearing from God in several ways, you're more apt to stay on the right track. What would we think of someone who only read his Bible for direction and never prayed? In the same way, those who pray for guidance without ever reading Scripture can easily fall into error.

Solomon wisely said, *"in the multitude of counselors there is safety"* (Proverbs 11:14). The apostle Paul echoed that truth in one of his epistles. *"By the mouth of two or three witnesses every word shall be established"* (2 Corinthians 13:1). If you're missing God's direction and you're not aware of it, God could use a dream to get through to you.

I can think of many examples like this. Once I ministered in a rural church. The wife of the music minister had developed a critical attitude toward the pastor. She even spoke about him in a derogatory way to others. Thinking her accusations were justified, she saw no reason to change. The same night that I taught on dreams, God clearly spoke to her during her sleep. The interpretation of the dream was obvious, and God exposed the rebellion in her heart. The next day, she anxiously told me what God had shown her. Had someone tried to correct her, she might not have received it. The dream broke through her deception, however, and she quickly repented of her critical attitude.

Once a retarded woman attended a church service where I taught on dreams. You might think that a retarded person shouldn't get involved with something so complex as receiving guidance in a dream. Actually, it turned out to be quite the opposite. She experienced a vivid dream that revealed her need to forgive her ex-husband who had left her for another woman. She promptly forgave him and rid herself of the destructive force of unforgiveness! The dream had cut through peripheral issues and showed her what was really in her heart.

Years ago, when I was stepping into full-time ministry, the Lord told me to resign my secular job. You need to know God's will when it comes to a major decision like that! I resigned, but my boss, being a very persuasive man, convinced me to accept more liberty with my working hours. His alternate plan seemed like a great idea.

That night, however, I had a dream. While driving down the highway, I missed my turn. Ahead I saw a place in the road where I could turn around to make the turn I had missed. When I woke up, it didn't take much prayer to figure out what God was saying. The next morning, I politely declined my employer's offer to stay. The dream confirmed that I was supposed to resign.

A woman came to me for help. Desperate to save her failing marriage, she had sought Christian counseling. After hearing her story, however, even a Christian counselor told her the marriage would probably never be restored. Confusion set in. Many of her friends discouraged her from even trying to salvage the relationship. Agonizing over an impending divorce, she asked my opinion. Even if I told her that her marriage could work, how could she know if I was right? Conflicting opinions caused her head to spin. As I searched the Word of God for advice, her situation seemed to be in a gray area.

I prayed with her, asking God to speak to her in a dream. Then she would know she had heard from God. That night she dreamed that she and her husband were building a beautiful stone house. They labored together, building it stone by stone. When she called me the next day, her voice reverberated with excitement. Now she knew their marriage could work. That's exactly what has been happening since her dream. She and her husband are working together to build a good marriage. Their relationship is working, and they know it will work because God spoke to her—in a dream!

As you read these accounts of dreams helping other people, can you think of an area in your own life where you're missing God? Do you need guidance for a particular situation, circumstance, or decision? God can use a dream to show that area to you. Dreams can certainly enhance your ability to hear from God.

God can give you direction, warning, and help in solving problems during the night season. Dreams can give you initial guidance as well as interim guidance. They can also confirm that you're on the right track. They can help you get back on the right track if you stray from God's will. You can turn night times into "hearing from God" times. You can learn to hear from God in dreams.

The same means of communication that God used to help Abimelech, Jacob, Joseph, a butler, Gideon, Nebuchadnezzar, Daniel, Pharaoh, Solomon, Nathan, Zechariah, the wise men, Joseph (Mary's husband), and others can help you today.

End-time saints of God, dreams can be an invaluable addition to your repertoire of ways to hear from Him! Come with me as we explore this wonderful means of hearing from God in the night season.

3

EQUIPPED FOR
A SAFE JOURNEY

One afternoon I went for a refreshing, brisk walk during a break in my seminar on how to hear the voice of God. As I meandered through a residential area near the church, a familiar prompting in my spirit told me, "Turn and walk down that road." Whenever these incidents occur, I raise my spiritual antennas and expect God to speak to me. My spiritual sensitivity heightened as I obeyed the prompting to change directions.

I noticed a young child, perhaps five or six years old, playing football with some older boys in a yard. While trying to tackle the ball carrier, this little fellow had gotten bowled over. The collision momentarily knocked the wind out of him, but then he caught his breath and began to cry. The others ran to where he was sprawled on the grass. They hoisted him to his feet, dusted him off, and made sure he wasn't hurt. In a few moments, he was back in the game.

A short distance away, I noticed a young girl who had just tumbled from her bicycle onto the asphalt. Cinders dug into her knee and the hand she used to break her fall. A friend brushed the cinders from her skin and gave her a hug. In a few moments she continued pedaling down the sidewalk.

That reminded me of the time when my own daughters were learning to ride their bicycles. When they lost their balance, fell off their bikes, and skinned their knees, my wife and I hurt almost as much as our girls did. After their first bad tumble, I was tempted to shelter them from all painful experiences. But I knew that they must grow, learn, and develop even if that involved some bumps and bruises.

As I pondered these incidents, the Lord showed me how easily we can shelter a young Christian from hurtful experiences. By discouraging them from taking risks, we can protect them. After seeing people hurt through incorrectly discerning God's voice, we may discourage others from moving in this realm. This is not God's plan, however. Jesus said, *"My sheep hear My voice, and I know them, and they follow Me"* (John 10:27). God wants to give us specific, timely guidance for our lives.

So what's the answer to this problem? Should we ignore the growth of young believers in the ways of the Spirit to prevent them from getting hurt? No, of course not. We must teach them spiritual truths in such a way that they can develop without falling into error or getting hurt by bad experiences. It can be done!

If I hiked up a steep trail before you journeyed on that same path, I could warn you about all the dangerous, tricky places that lay before you. You could avoid a sudden turn or drop where you might trip. My previous experience would help you greatly. That's why this chapter is so important.

Explorers thrive on adventure, but they don't jeopardize their safety. Mountain climbers equip themselves to minimize the risks associated with high altitudes, inclement weather, and treacherous terrain. You're about to embark on an adventure in hearing from God. Don't rush off without putting on the safety gear found in this chapter. I'll show you how to keep from getting hurt by using the following six safeguards:

1. Be cautious as you learn to receive guidance in dreams.

2. Do not rely on dreams alone for guidance, especially when making major decisions and when first learning to hear from God in this manner.

3. God often uses familiar terms to speak to you about spiritual things.

4. Most dreams should not be taken literally.

5. Do not allow confusion or fear to overwhelm you as the result of a dream.

6. Guidance received through a God-given dream will never contradict the counsel of the written Word of God.

Let's look at each of these safeguards in detail.

Be Cautious!

Several years ago I taught on dreams in a church in Texas. That very night a young man in the congregation dreamed he was going to California. The morning after he had the dream, he packed his bags and went! I never found out if he missed God or not. My experience tells me that he had a good opportunity to miss God because he moved with such haste.

When a young Christian discovers a new truth, his zeal can cause him to act prematurely. These uninformed believers do not understand that God has a speed limit. In the same way that a motorist finds signs to direct him as he drives, an alert believer will find that God places signs in his path for spiritual direction. God gives warning signs, direction signs, stop signs, and even speed limit signs.

Many times in my ministry God has told me to slow down; at other times He encouraged me to move faster. As you begin to act on the guidance received from God in dreams—or in any other way that's new to you—remember the speed limit. Move slowly, *especially* when following guidance received from dreams.

As you begin to hear from God in the night season, you'll probably receive a dream and easily get the interpretation. You might say, "This is easy! I've got it!" and begin to base decisions on the dreams you receive. Don't get too confident as you're learning.

One of my friends is an expert pilot who has logged over 12,000 hours of flight time. I trust him to fly me anywhere. Once, when we were flying across the Texas skies, he told me something I've never forgotten:

> The most dangerous pilot is not one who's just starting to fly. The most dangerous is one who has a hundred or so hours and is overconfident. Often he doesn't have enough respect for the weather or for the mechanical condition of the plane. He takes unnecessary, dangerous chances.

Believers who begin to hear from God in dreams can also become overconfident. Don't become puffed up by your initial success in interpreting dreams, and don't take unnecessary chances.

Dreams can be complex in nature. Like developing skill in any vocation, one starts with the basics and learns more complex aspects with time and experience. Although the newest believer can hear from God in dreams, skillfulness and proficiency are developed over a period of time.

As you grow in your understanding of dreams, God will often give you simple dreams and gradually develop your understanding of more complex ones. You must crawl before you can walk. And you must walk before you can run.

You should also be cautious in how you share your expeditions into the world of dreams. After Daniel received a perplexing vision, he said, "*but I kept the matter in my heart*" (Daniel 7:28). Joseph, who was already the envy of his brothers, would have benefited from this advice. How did his family respond to his dreams?

Now Joseph dreamed a dream, and he told it to his brothers; and they hated him even more. So he said to them, "Please hear this dream which I have dreamed: There we were, binding sheaves in the field. Then behold, my sheaf arose and also stood upright; and indeed your sheaves stood all around and bowed down to my sheaf." And his brothers said to him, "Shall you indeed reign over us? Or shall you indeed have dominion over us?" So they hated him even more for his dreams and for his words. Then he dreamed still another dream and told it to his brothers, and said, "Look, I have dreamed another dream. And this time, the sun, the moon, and the eleven stars bowed down to me." So he told it to his father and his brothers; and his father rebuked him and said to him, "What is this dream that you have dreamed? Shall your mother and I and your brothers indeed come to bow down to the earth before you?" And his brothers envied him, but his father kept the matter in mind. (Genesis 37:5–11)

Joseph's grandiose dreams provoked jealousy and strife in his family. Use discretion in sharing your experiences with others. Learning to hear from God in a fresh, new way should always encourage others to draw closer to the Lord.

Hear from God in Many Ways

God is a God of many voices. He speaks in a variety of ways. (See Hebrews 1:1,2.) If you rely on dreams alone for guidance, you're opening yourself to deception and error. Scripture says that "*a dream comes through much activity*" (Ecclesiastes 5:3). Maybe your dream sprang from the activity of your day. Scripture also admonishes us, "*Neither hearken to your dreams which ye cause to be dreamed*" (Jeremiah 29:8, KJV). You need to be sure you're following only God-given dreams.

How can we be sure that we're discerning God's voice? This leads to our second rule: *Do not rely on dreams alone for guidance, especially when making major decisions and when first learning to hear from God in this manner.*

Unlike the young man who moved to California, I wouldn't make such an important decision on the basis of one dream. I would seek God for other pieces to confirm His direction. Are you seeking God's will about a large financial investment, a career move, or your marriage partner? You can walk in safety by hearing from Him in more than one way. If God is speaking, all of His ways of communicating will line up to confirm His will.

God used this principle to convince Peter that Gentiles as well as Jews would inherit salvation. God directed Peter in the following ways to lead him to his conclusion:

1. A vision during prayer. "*I was in the city of Joppa praying; and in a trance I saw a vision*" (Acts 11:5).

2. A word spoken to him by the Holy Spirit. "*While Peter thought about the vision, the Spirit said to him, 'Behold, three men are seeking you'*" (Acts 10:19).

3. The arrival of three men who asked for him. "*At that very moment, three men stood before the house where I was, having been sent to me from Caesarea*" (Acts 11:11).

4. The testimony of a devout man. "*And [Cornelius] told us how he had seen an angel standing in his house, who said to him, 'Send men to Joppa, and call for Simon whose surname is Peter, who will tell you words by which you and all your household will be saved'*" (Acts 11:13–14).

5. The demonstration of signs and wonders. *"While Peter was still speaking these words, the Holy Spirit fell upon all those who heard the word. And those of the circumcision who believed were astonished, as many as came with Peter, because the gift of the Holy Spirit had been poured out on the Gentiles also"* (Acts 10:44–45).

6. Remembering the Word of God. *"Then I remembered the word of the Lord, how He said, 'John indeed baptized with water, but you shall be baptized with the Holy Spirit'"* (Acts 11:16).

Do you see it? God spoke in a variety of ways to Peter. When he put all the pieces together, Peter knew he had heard from God! All the information led to the same conclusion.

After Peter received the revelation that God was pouring out His Spirit upon the Gentiles as well as the Jews, he shared it with the brethren. When they preached to the Gentiles, they experienced the same results. The confirmations proved that Peter had heard from God.

Although this example involved understanding a vision received while in a trance during prayer, it still demonstrates one of the principal benefits of hearing from God in dreams. Dreams fit together with the other ways in which God speaks to assure you that you really are hearing from God. God can use dreams to give initial guidance, interim guidance, and confirmations.

1. *Initial guidance.* When he was seventeen years old, Joseph received dreams that one day he would hold a position of authority over his parents and brothers. (See Genesis 37:5-11.)

2. *Interim guidance.* Jacob received a dream that God would bless him with many descendants and bring him back to Bethel. (See Genesis 28:12-22.) After serving his uncle

Laban for twenty years, Jacob received another dream that directed him to return to his father's land. (See Genesis 31:11-13.)

3. *Confirmations.* Gideon lacked confidence that God could use him to rout the Midianites. A dream bolstered his faith in God. (See Judges 7:9-15.)

You need to develop skill in hearing from God in the variety of ways that He speaks, including dreams. The different ways fit together, like pieces of a puzzle, to give you the whole picture of what He is saying. Dreams are important pieces to the puzzle, but not the only pieces.

As you develop your skill in hearing from God in all the different ways through which He speaks, you greatly increase your ability to stay in tune with God continually. You can receive constant guidance from Him about your job, marriage, finances, and ministry.

Many Christians miss a large percentage of the communication that He sends to them because they lack skill in recognizing and receiving communication from God. This deficiency need not exist in your life, however. You can be very adept in hearing from God in all of the ways through which He speaks—including dreams.

God Uses the Familiar

When God called me into full-time ministry years ago, I learned some valuable truths about hearing from Him. While seeking God for direction for my life, I received a dream in which I was working for an insurance company that had previously employed me. I assumed that God wanted me to return to that company, which had moved to Baton Rouge, Louisiana.

I called the company to inquire about a sales position, and they were interested in hiring me. I set up an appointment, drove four hours to Baton Rouge, and ate lunch with one of the vice-presidents. He gave me their materials, rate book, and other necessary tools to get started.

I drove back to my hometown of Beaumont, Texas, where I tried to sell insurance. Nothing seemed to work. Finally, after three long and fruitless weeks, I realized that I had misinterpreted my dream. Still learning to hear from God in the night season, I had moved too hastily.

That experience taught me an expensive, painful, and unforgettable lesson. I also discovered that the dream was giving me direction in the *ministry,* not the insurance business. This led me to our next God-given principle: *God often uses familiar terms to speak to you about spiritual things.* If you dream about your job, it may mean your job, or it may mean something else entirely.

Jesus told His disciples, who were fishermen, *"Follow Me, and I will make you fishers of men"* (Matthew 4:19, emphasis added). He used fishermen's terms to talk to them about evangelism. Use caution as you develop your skill in receiving guidance from God-given dreams. The language of dreams is largely symbolic and can be easily misinterpreted.

I wish someone had guided me when I was first learning to receive God-inspired dreams. Godly counsel would have spared me from making many mistakes. Let me share another example where God spoke to me with familiar terms, but I misinterpreted His use of symbols.

Missing God 's Signals

God called me into the ministry when I was managing a casualty insurance agency. He directed me to resign that position and then take a job selling life insurance on a commission basis only. This gave me freedom to pursue the ministry while meeting my needs through selling insurance.

During this time, God gave me a dream. When I had been in the life insurance business earlier in my life, I had passed five parts of the C.L.U. (Chartered Life Underwriter) course in insurance. The C.L.U. designation, much like the C.P.A. title in accounting, is a professional designation earned through passing ten segments of a comprehensive study program in insurance. I had no desire to complete the remainder of the C.L.U. program. I wanted to become a minister. Then came the dream.

I dreamed that I was holding a photo album. As I opened the album, the picture on the left showed a group of men in the insurance business. I was also in the picture. As I looked at the picture on the right, I saw another group of men. I didn't recognize any of them, and I wasn't in this picture. One of the men in this picture was dressed like a priest. Above the pictures I saw the letters B.B.B.–C.L.U. I knew the letters stood for "Better Business Bureau, Chartered Life Underwriter." As I woke up, I thought I needed to get my C.L.U. designation to do better in business.

As I contemplated all the work involved in passing the rest of the exams, dread overwhelmed me. Furthermore, it meant that I would be selling insurance for a longer period of time than I had anticipated. Determined to obey God, however, I took steps to enroll in the C.L.U. courses.

Then I had another dream in which family members brought me presents on my birthday. Each present was a communication device. One brought me a radio. Another brought me a microphone. Still another brought me a telephone. What a weird dream! I didn't understand it, so I simply recorded the dream and dated it.

Then strange events began to happen! Everywhere I went, members of the body of Christ told me that they felt God had called me to preach. This occurred at least eight times in a period of two weeks. Each time it happened, I told them that I agreed. First, however, I was to get my C.L.U. designation in insurance because God had instructed me to do so. I was sure I had heard from God.

Another Piece of the Puzzle

Not long after that, I dreamed that a man was in jail because of an alcohol problem. I visited him, gave him a message from God, and prayed for him. Then I woke up. What in the world could that dream mean? Would I be ministering to someone in jail? Again, I didn't understand the dream, so I merely wrote it down in the composition book that I keep by my bedside.

I went to my office that morning as usual. While I worked at my desk, the phone rang. A member of my church called. "Brother Benny," she said, "a friend of mine got picked up for drunk driving last night, and he's in jail. The pastor is out of town. Can you visit him?"

Immediately I remembered the dream I had received that morning. "Yes," I enthusiastically replied, "I'll be glad to visit him!" How exciting! God had given me a message for this man in a dream that very morning. I went to my car and quickly drove to the county jail.

Upon arriving at the jail, I got out of my car and walked into the receptionist's office. "May I help you?" she asked.

"Yes," I responded, "I'm here to visit this man." I handed her a piece of paper with the man's name written on it. "Someone in my church requested that I visit him," I said. Knowing I had a message for the man, I bubbled over with excitement. Then the receptionist threw me a curve.

"Are you a licensed minister?"

"No. Our pastor is out of town, but I frequently minister in his behalf when he's absent."

"I'm sorry, sir, but you cannot visit this man unless you are a licensed minister."

"But you don't understand," I told her. "*I know* I'm supposed to visit this man."

"I'm sorry, sir, but you absolutely cannot get in without a valid minister's license."

I was stunned! I thought that God would make a way for me to get in. Hadn't He given me a message for this man? What went wrong? As I drove home, discouragement and confusion settled over me. After pulling into the driveway, I decided to mow the grass. I quickly changed clothes, went outside, and started the lawn mower. As I pushed the mower back and forth across the back yard, I rehearsed the different events that had occurred in recent days.

Why would God give me a message for this man and then close the door for me to deliver it? As I continued to mow and ponder, I thought about the birthday party dream. Right after I had the dream, different members of the body of Christ began to give me the same message. God was calling me to be a minister. Then the woman at the jail told me I needed a minister's license. Yet, I was so sure about the meaning of the C.L.U. dream. It seemed so clear.

I decided to read the C.L.U. dream again. Perhaps I had overlooked some piece of it. I stopped the mower and went inside. I got my composition book and found the page where I had recorded the dream about getting my C.L.U. title. As I read the dream, one piece suddenly made sense for the first time. In describing the picture on the right, I had simply stated, "One man was dressed like a priest."

Then I saw it! God had given me an analogy. Just as I would get my professional designation if I were pursuing an insurance career, I needed to get my professional designation to be in the ministry. God wanted me to become a licensed minister! Thank God, I wasn't going to have to take that C.L.U. training after all! Instead, I enrolled in a Bible college course and became a licensed minister, a title that I was much more enthusiastic about obtaining.

This lesson taught me to be cautious when interpreting dreams, and it also emphasized another important principle that I had begun to learn: *Most dreams should not be taken literally.* This is a very important rule. Please refrain from interpreting your dreams literally. You'll avoid a lot of confusion, bad decisions, and heartache. How should you interpret dreams? That brings us to the next point.

Learn to Think Symbolically

The language of dreams is highly symbolic. Study the dreams and visions recorded in Scripture if you doubt this. Thinking symbolically requires time and conditioning, but you must train yourself to do this. Dreams in the Bible nearly always required interpretation.

> *And they* [Pharaoh's officers] *said to* [Joseph], *"We each have dreamed a dream, and there is no interpreter of it." And Joseph said to them,* **"Do not interpretations belong to God?"** (Genesis 40:8, emphasis added)

> *This is the dream. Now we will tell the* **interpretation** *of it before the king.* (Daniel 2:36, emphsis added)

*And so it was, when Gideon heard the telling of the dream and **its interpretation**, that he worshiped. He returned to the camp of Israel, and said, "Arise, for the* LORD *has delivered the camp of Midian in-to your hand."*

(Judges 7:15, emphasis added)

The Holy Spirit uses symbolic language in visions and dreams. Throughout the Bible God shows a symbol or picture and gives the interpretation to the symbol. The different pieces or symbols given in a dream have meanings or interpretations. Gideon overheard a man telling his dream, and his companion gave the interpretation.

And when Gideon had come, there was a man telling a dream to his companion. He said, "I have just had a dream: To my surprise, a loaf of barley bread tumbled into the camp of Midian; it came to a tent and struck it so that it fell and over-turned, and the tent collapsed." (Judges 7:13)

If we were to take this dream literally, then an actual loaf of bread would tumble into the camp of the Midianites and knock over a tent. Of course, this was not the meaning. The interpretation of the symbols is found in the next verse.

His companion answered and said, "This is nothing else but the sword of Gideon the son of Joash, a man of Israel; for into his hand God has delivered Midian and the whole camp."

(Judges 7:14)

As you begin to receive dreams, you'll have a natural inclination to interpret your dreams literally. Dreams often seem so real—especially when you first wake up. After a few days have passed, you'll find it easier to understand the symbols and interpret the dream symbolically.

Can God give a literal dream? I'm sure He can. I've heard testimonies of such occurrences. Most dreams, however, require interpretations. In my opinion, the safest rule is to think symbolically. I can only speak from my own experience and the Word of God. All dreams in the Bible required interpretations unless a message came in the dream from an angel. Sometimes, if a message is given in words (as opposed to symbols), that message may be literal. Even in dreams, the bearer of the message may have a symbolic meaning. Otherwise, it's best to think in symbolic terms.

Let's look at another example that combines the use of symbolism with an important warning. *Do not allow confusion or fear to overwhelm you as the result of a dream.*

Fear Not!

Several years ago my wife and I were on a ministry tour in Nebraska. During the second night of the tour, she experienced a vivid dream. In the dream, she walked into the bathroom of our home in Texas and discovered that our teenage daughter had drowned in the bathtub. She tried to revive her, but to no avail. Then my wife ran into the bedroom where her mother was and screamed, "Help me pray! Jodie has drowned, and I can't revive her!" Then my wife awoke. Needless to say, the dream frightened her.

"Don't panic," I told her. "Let's pray and ask God for the interpretation." As we prayed, the Lord showed me that our daughter represented my wife's faith in regard to buying a motor home for our ministry trips. For two years our family frequently lived out of a van during these tours. My wife had grown weary of the cramped quarters. Her faith had literally died because we had been unable to purchase a motor home. Her mother symbolized the Holy Spirit, whom she asked to help her pray.

Why did God use our daughter to represent my wife's faith? Because my wife's faith for the motor home, like our daughter, had nearly grown to maturity. You can let your faith die in the early stages or in the later stages, can't you?

Sure enough, my wife confirmed that was exactly what she was going through! Then we stood against unbelief, and my wife spent some time praying in the Holy Spirit. Her faith responded, and just one week later we heard about a fantastic deal on a motor home. We bought it, and my wife saw the manifestation of the long-awaited promise!

Had we taken this dream literally, we would have feared for our daughter's life! Like most dreams, hers was symbolic. As her faith approached maturity in an area, it suffered a setback. In fact, it died. Thank God, we were able to resurrect it and see the promise come to life! God sent the dream to help us!

This incident simply re-emphasizes why Christians need to develop wisdom in dream interpretation—a valid means of hearing from God. I can imagine the response of some people if they had heard about my wife's dream:

"It was a nightmare."

"It was just your imagination."

"It was from the devil."

"You better pray for your daughter. God is warning you that her life is in danger."

"Did you eat pizza before you went to bed?"

Let's stamp out ignorance in these areas and press in to benefit from God-given direction in dreams.

After receiving a vivid dream like the one my wife had, many people experience fear or confusion as they wake up. Scary plots, evil characters, and chase scenes in dreams can shake anyone's composure. Don't allow yourself to be tormented by a dream. If you give place to fear or confusion, you open yourself to these unclean spirits. That's not God's will for your life!

> *God has not given us a spirit of fear, but of power and of love and of a sound mind.* (2 Timothy 1:7)

> *For God is not the author of confusion but of peace.* (1 Corinthians 14:33)

If you succumb to this frame of mind, it will interfere with your ability to hear from God. Even if you receive a dream as a warning, its purpose is to help you—not to confuse or scare you.

I had a dream that puzzled me. Afraid that I wouldn't figure out the warning in time, I opened myself to torment. Feeding those fearful thoughts only made me feel worse. Sure enough, I went through a difficult experience, and I made some mistakes. The dream had been a warning, but I didn't understand it enough to avoid the situation. But do you know what? Jesus got me through the situation anyway. He's good at that, isn't He?

Being hampered by fear certainly didn't help me, did it? If anything, it worked against my being able to hear from God. I learned an important lesson from it. Don't give in to fear! Don't give in to confusion! Trust God instead.

Is It Consistent with Scripture?

The next guideline not only applies to hearing from God in dreams, but also would apply to hearing from God in any way through which He speaks. *Guidance received through a God-given dream will never contradict the overall counsel of the written Word of God.*

Any direction that you receive that encourages you to sin or violate the precepts found in the Bible is erroneous, and you should not follow it. God warned His people about "dreamers of dreams" that might lead them astray.

If there arises among you a prophet or a dreamer of dreams, and he gives you a sign or a wonder, and the sign or the wonder comes to pass, of which he spoke to you, saying, "Let us go after other gods which you have not known, and let us serve them," you shall not listen to the words of that prophet or that dreamer of dreams, for the LORD your God is testing you to know whether you love the LORD your God with all your heart and with all your soul. You shall walk after the LORD your God and fear Him, and keep His commandments and obey His voice, and you shall serve Him and hold fast to Him.   (Deuteronomy 13:1–4)

People have fallen into sin because they believed they were being led by the Spirit of God even though the guidance they were following clearly contradicted the Word of God.

I knew a Christian woman who wanted to divorce her husband. Actually, she wanted to marry a minister she had met. She convinced herself that God told her to divorce her husband. Many of her friends tried to tell her that she was wrong, but she refused to listen. She severed her fellowship with the body of Christ, and she stopped reading the Bible. She stubbornly believed that God wanted her to leave her husband when she had no scriptural reason for it.

Finally, the divorce went through. Then she secretly began to see the minister who was married and had a large family. He subsequently divorced his wife and married my friend. Devastation came to both of their lives. The man lost his church and his ministry. The new marriage didn't work out. My friend fell into worse sin and error because she chose to ignore the best discerning tool that God has given His people—the written Word of God!

For the word of God is living and powerful, and sharper than any two-edged sword, piercing even to the division of soul and spirit, and of joints and marrow, and is a discerner of the thoughts and intents of the heart. (Hebrews 4:12)

Whether we're accepting the counsel of a friend, discerning what we've heard in prayer, or pondering the meaning of a dream, we must check all guidance against the written Word of God.

We've covered the basic rules to keep you on solid ground as you begin to learn to hear from God in dreams. Let's summarize the guidelines found in this chapter:

1. Be cautious as you learn to receive guidance in dreams.

2. Do not rely on dreams alone for guidance, especially when making major decisions and when first learning to hear from God in this manner.

3. God often uses familiar terms to speak to you about spiritual things.

4. Most dreams should not be taken literally.

5. Do not allow confusion or fear to overwhelm you as the result of a dream.

6. Guidance received through a God-given dream will never contradict the counsel of the written Word of God.

Now that we know what safety gear to wear, let's continue our journey. Next, we must unlock a large gate in order to step across the threshold into the world of dreams. Shall we check it out? Let's go!

4

UNLOCKING THE GATE

When I was a very young Christian, I attended a church service where the pastor opened the meeting with brief testimonies. During this time, a young lady stood up and shared that God had spoken to her in a dream.

What? My ears perked up. Did I hear her right? Does God really speak to people in dreams? As I thought about God personally communicating to me in a dream, my spirit leaped with excitement. As soon as I got home that night, I knelt beside my bed and talked to God.

"Lord," I asked, "is it really true that You talk to people in dreams? If so, please talk to me in a dream tonight. And if You would, please tell me how to walk in the Spirit. You know that has been my constant, fervent prayer."

After that simple prayer, I crawled into bed and drifted off to sleep with a sense of anticipation in my spirit. As I woke up the next morning, I realized that I had just experienced a very vivid dream.

In the dream, I was driving my car down the highway. Then the engine began to run roughly and to miss. In fact, it got worse and worse until I finally pulled onto the shoulder of the road.

Then, just as I rolled to a stop, the engine died. I got out of the car and lifted the hood. As I surveyed the engine, my heart sunk with grief. The engine was completely burned up! The water had leaked out and caused the engine to overheat! I felt sick!

Then I woke up. As I pondered the dream, my first reaction was to take the dream literally. Was God warning me about overheating my car? I checked the radiator, and the water level was fine. As I soaked in a hot bath that morning, pondering the dream, revelation began to drift into my thoughts.

The car represented my life. Just as the gauges of a car enable the driver to check the condition of the engine, several spiritual barometers enable a person to evaluate his walk with the Lord. Had I charged my spiritual battery by spending time in prayer? Was I full of the Word, or empty? Was I overflowing with the oil of gladness? Just as the engine of a car should be regularly maintained and serviced, so should my spiritual walk. Regularly checking my spiritual gauges could prevent me from grieving the Holy Spirit. God had answered my prayer and was teaching me how to walk in the Spirit.

It's So Simple!

Since God wants you to be sure that you're following Him, He will work with you to prove that He's speaking to you in dreams. He will personally demonstrate to you the validity of dreams for today. God said, *"Test all things; hold fast what is good"* (1 Thessalonians 5:21).

Once He demonstrates it to you, then you should learn to receive dreams in the night season. Ask God to speak to you. Remind Him of all of the Scriptures we've already discussed. Ask Him for a demonstration. He is able to back up His Word! He wants you to know His voice!

Remember, in the last days, we shall *"dream dreams"* (Joel 2:28; Acts 2:17).

It's in the Bible!

It's for today!

And it's for *you* today!

Receiving a dream from God is so simple. You've already seen that it's a sign of God pouring out His Spirit in the last days. Now it's up to Him to demonstrate to you that it's real. Let me give you some simple keys to help you learn to receive dreams from God. I'll support each point with Scripture.

1. Ask God to speak to you in dreams.

2. Expect to receive.

3. When you wake up, be still for a moment and see if you can recall a dream.

4. Record each dream and date it.

Let's look at these in detail.

Ask God to Speak to You

When I first began to receive dreams from God, I unintentionally followed a biblical pattern that enables us to receive all that God has for us. Someone testified that God spoke to them in a dream. Having heard that, I simply prayed and asked God to speak to me that way—and He did!

"Ask, and you will receive" (John 16:24).

Yes, that's right!

You must receive dreams!

This key unlocks the main entry gate into the world of dreams. In fact, we enjoy all God's blessings by asking for them in faith and receiving the promises. Think about the tremendous spiritual blessings God has stored up for us: salvation, healing, spiritual gifts, and the baptism in the Holy Spirit. None of these wonderful things just happen in someone's life, do they?

Scripture tells us how people receive salvation. *"Faith comes by hearing, and hearing by the word of God"* (Romans 10:17). How did you get saved? You heard the Gospel, and you received it by faith.

This same principle applies to hearing from God in dreams. People don't know they can have this manifestation in their life, so they don't experience it. Many people have never received a dream from God because they've never asked Him for one. Scripture says, *"You do not have because you do not ask"* (James 4:2). You must seek to hear from God in the night season.

Some people think that if God wants them to have a dream, it will just happen sovereignly. Those people don't get many dreams from God. Remember that God made some very specific promises:

> *Ask, and it will be given to you; seek, and you will find; knock, and it will be opened to you. For everyone who asks receives, and he who seeks finds, and to him who knocks it will be opened. Or what man is there among you who, if his son asks for bread, will give him a stone? Or if he asks for a fish, will he give him a serpent? If you then, being evil, know how to give good gifts to your children, how much more will your Father who is in heaven give good things to those who ask Him!*   (Matthew 7:7–11, emphasis added)

Some Christians have told me they've been taught to never seek dreams. I can understand why they were taught that, too! People have been hurt through abuses and error. That's why we've already discussed safeguards. People may incorrectly interpret dreams or use poor judgment, but dreams are still a valid way to hear from God.

A woman who attended my seminar on hearing from God was reluctant to ask God to speak to her in dreams. Not wanting to do anything that might be wrong, she told God how she felt. Despite her previous instruction, she asked God to prove Himself to her in this way.

The next afternoon she lay down for a nap and soon drifted off to sleep. Upon awakening from the nap, she lay still for a moment and tried to recall a dream, and behold—there was one! The dream concerned her son. As she prayed over it, she also received the interpretation. God revealed some very pertinent information about the way she had been handling her son's behavior. The dream helped her tremendously. As a matter of fact, the dream enabled God to get through to her when He hadn't been able to get through to her in other ways. Now she's an avid listener in the night (or nap) season!

It's perfectly all right to ask God to speak to you in a variety of scriptural ways—including dreams and visions. God can speak to us about specific situations through His Word. Isn't it all right to pray for this before you open your Bible? Many times God has spoken to me through a message at church. Isn't it all right to ask God to speak to you before you arrive for the service? God also communicates to men through dreams and visions. We can trust Him to speak to us in these scriptural ways, especially if we ask Him to confirm His direction.

You need to be hungry to hear from God in all of the ways that He speaks. Since becoming a Christian, I've always hungered to know the ways of God. For years my constant prayer was to "walk in His Spirit, hear His voice, and do His will." Late at night when I was unable to sleep, I often sought the Lord in my office at home. As I paced back and forth, praying in the Spirit, my prayers were interspersed with my petition, "God, I want to walk in Your Spirit, hear Your voice, and do Your will."

You need a deep hunger for God and His ways, too. Perhaps you already have it; perhaps you don't. But you need to cultivate it if you really want to benefit from the message in this book. If you lack that hunger for God, you must develop it. Pray for it. Tell your spirit to be filled with a hunger for godly things. Act like you already have it by seeking God in prayer and in the Word. Set aside time to seek God with fasting. If you do these things, sooner or later the hunger will appear.

Expect to Receive

Expectancy is a form of faith. All too often we're surprised when God speaks to us or intervenes in our lives. Knowing the nature of God, we should *expect* these things to happen. Jesus said, *"My sheep hear My voice"* (John 10:27). Hearing from God should be the norm and not the exception for Christians. Let's look at an example of expectancy in the Scriptures.

> *A woman who had a flow of blood for twelve years came from behind and touched the hem of His garment; for she said to herself, "If only I may touch His garment, I shall be made well." But Jesus turned around, and when He saw her He said, "Be of good cheer, daughter; your faith has made you well." And the woman was made well from that hour.*
> (Matthew 9:20–22)

The key verse tells us, *"she said to herself…"* She *expected* to be healed when she touched His garment! That expectancy caused her faith to draw the power of God.

Your expectancy will help you receive from God. As soon as you ask God to speak to you in dreams, you should place a notebook and a pen on your nightstand. Remember that faith without works is dead. (See James 2:17.) This simple act releases your faith and shows God that you're expecting to receive from Him in the night season!

Expectancy makes a big difference in what we receive from God. Let's look at another scriptural example.

*Now Peter and John went up together to the temple at the hour of prayer, the ninth hour. And a certain man lame from his mother's womb was carried, whom they laid daily at the gate…to ask alms from those who entered the temple; who, seeing Peter and John about to go into the temple, asked for alms. And fixing his eyes on him, with John, Peter said, "Look at us." So he gave them his attention, **expecting to receive something from them.** Then Peter said, "Silver and gold I do not have, but what I do have I give you: In the name of Jesus Christ of Nazareth, rise up and walk." And he took him by the right hand and lifted him up, and immediately his feet and ankle bones received strength. So he, leaping up, stood and walked and entered the temple with them—walking, leaping, and praising God.*   (Acts 3:1–9, emphasis added)*

Many times I've seen this principle demonstrated when I pray for the sick. Those who come to God with an attitude of expectancy frequently receive their healings with ease. A woman who had suffered with a cantaloupe-size tumor in her mid-section came to receive healing. As I scanned the prayer line, the Holy Spirit pointed her out to me. As she waited for God's healing touch, her countenance beamed with anticipation. Finally, she stepped to the front of the prayer line.

"Do you believe God will do this for you?" I asked.

"*I know* He will!" she replied with confidence.

"Receive your healing in Jesus' name!" I said as I stretched my hand toward her. I never even touched her. The power of God immediately dissolved her tumor.

"Praise the Lord! I'm healed!" she declared. That woman got exactly what she expected from God. And you'll get exactly what you expect to receive from God in the night season.

Try to Recall Your Dreams

In order to hear from God in dreams, you must ask Him to speak to you this way. You must expect God to give you dreams. But you must also *receive*. Scripture says, *"Ask, and you will receive"* (John 16:24). How do you receive a dream that occurs when you're not in control of what's going on? We can find the answer in Scripture.

> Now the angel who talked with me came back and wakened
> me, as a man who is wakened out of his sleep. And he said to
> me, "What do you see?" So I said, "I am looking, and there is
> a lampstand of solid gold...."   (Zechariah 4:1–2)

Do you see it? Zechariah was awakened "as a man who is awakened out of his sleep." As soon as he awakened, the angel asked, "What do you see?" Zechariah responded with a significant detail to remembering your dreams. He said, *"I am **looking**, and there is a lampstand of solid gold"* (Zechariah 4:2, emphasis added).

Here's the point you need to understand. *Zechariah did not see the lampstand until he looked!* This is why many people don't receive the direction that God sends to them in the night season. They don't look! The angel reminded Zechariah to look. I'm reminding you. When you wake up, before you do anything else, *look!*

When you wake up, ask yourself, Could God have awakened me? As soon as you realize you're awake, try to recall a dream from your memory. Sometimes it may be vivid; other dreams may appear faint or dim. You may recall only a little piece at first. As you meditate on that piece, other pieces may come back to you. Then you can recreate the dream in its entirety.

As you learn to receive dreams from God, you'll often wake up at the very end of a dream. The timing of your awakening will be perfect. That's the time to look in your memory and see if you can recall a dream.

You may seem to have awakened naturally. As natural as it may seem, however, you may have been awakened supernaturally! Scripture says, *"For in Him we live and move and have our being"* (Acts 17:28). Have you ever considered that in Him you live and move and wake up?

God showed me that *He* often woke me up in the night season. When I woke up, I glanced at the digital clock on my nightstand, and it was 3:33 a.m. This happened not just once but many times. Finally, I realized that it wasn't coincidence. It was God. I seemed to wake up naturally, but God actually woke me up!

Once God awakened me in a very unusual way. At first, however, I didn't realize it was God! A fly buzzed around my face and aroused me from sleep. I awoke and slapped at the fly with my hand. The following night I couldn't believe that a fly was buzzing around my face again. As I woke up, however, I realized there was no fly. I had been hearing the fly in my sleep, but he wasn't really there.

Then God spoke to me!

"I sent that fly last night to wake you up."

Preposterous? Not really. Don't laugh. Give God a little credit! He can use His creatures for His purpose, can't He? Remember, He used a plant and a worm to speak to Jonah. (See Jonah 4:6-11.) The writer of Proverbs admonishes us through the actions of an ant. (See Proverbs 6:6–11.) God can use one of His insects as an instrument to do His will.

Actually, I learned a very important principle from this lesson. Very often the things that happen in a perfectly natural manner are actually God-inspired happenings. Sometimes when you seem to awaken naturally, you're really being awakened supernaturally. Even if you were awakened by a noise, perhaps it wasn't an accident! When you wake up unexpectedly, watch and listen for God. See if you can recall a dream.

Today, many families own video recorders. My wife and I think the best feature is the preset function. If we want to record a television program while we're out for the evening, we pre-set it to record a certain program at a certain time.

If man can devise a machine capable of stopping at the end of a television program, how much more can God wake us precisely at the end of a dream? If God gives you a dream, then He knows when it starts and when it ends. That's the reason you'll often wake up immediately after a dream. With a little effort, you can rewind it and replay it while it is fresh in your memory.

Record and Date the Dream

Many people ignore my next piece of advice for a variety of reasons. Perhaps it's too much trouble, or perhaps it just doesn't seem that important. Bypassing this step, however, will cause you to lose key guidance from God.

If you're a serious student of wanting to hear from God in dreams, then you *must* form a habit of always writing down and dating the things you receive in the night season! This is a scriptural practice.

> *In the first year of Belshazzar king of Babylon, Daniel had a dream and visions of his head while on his bed. Then* **he wrote down the dream, telling the main facts.**
> (Daniel 7:1, emphasis added)

Some dreams are very vivid; others are faint. Both can contain anointed counsel from God. But even the most vivid dreams can be forgotten by morning. If you really want to hear God in the night season, you must record your dreams. Scripture says that some dreams are very memorable—even pulling our emotions into play.

The multitude...shall be as a dream of a night vision. It shall even be as when a hungry man dreams, and look—he eats; but he awakes, and his soul is still empty; or as when a thirsty man dreams, and look—he drinks; but he awakes, and indeed he is faint, and his soul still craves.   (Isaiah 29:7, 8)

Can you imagine being famished and your dream about eating is so real that you wake up? That's a vivid dream!

People have told me, "Brother, I had a dream last night, and I know it was from God because it was so vivid!" Many dreams that *aren't* vivid also come from God. Sometimes the things of the Spirit of God are faint. That's why we need to cultivate spiritual sensitivity.

When God rebuked Aaron and Miriam for speaking against Moses, He implied that dreams could be an obscure means of communication.

*If there is a prophet among you, I, the LORD, make Myself known to him in a vision, and I speak to him in a dream. Not so with My servant Moses....I speak with him face to face, even plainly, and not in **dark sayings.***
(Numbers 12:6–8, emphasis added)

Dreams can be perplexing, disturbing, and fleeting. King Nebuchadnezzar had just such a dream from God. As he recounted his experience, he stated that his sleep left him.

Now in the second year of Nebuchadnezzar's reign, Nebuchadnezzar had dreams; and his spirit was so troubled that his sleep left him. (Daniel 2:1)

What was significant about Nebuchadnezzar's dream? He couldn't remember it! *"The king answered and said to the Chaldeans, The thing is gone from me"* (Daniel 2:5 KJV, emphasis added). Obviously, Nebuchadnezzar's dream was not very vivid and not easy to remember. Some dreams are very vivid and easy to recall upon awakening. Some are not. God can use either kind to convey an important message.

One night I woke up after having a vivid dream. I knew I would remember it because it was so clear. Just to be sure, however, I rehearsed it in my mind until I couldn't possibly forget it. Then I drifted back to sleep. You guessed it! When I woke up the next morning, I couldn't pull the dream from my memory. I lost it!

God's Word warns us that dreams can be quite elusive. *"He will fly away like a dream, and not be found; yes, he will be chased away like a vision of the night"* (Job 20:8). I've lost many precious insights, songs, and dreams in the night season because I thought I could remember them without writing them down. I've learned to carry my composition book with me whenever I travel. I find it best always to be ready to write down what God may give to me.

God may give you guidance in a dream that won't apply for weeks, months, or even years. Daniel's visions pertained to an era thousands of years into the future. (See Daniel 8:17; 10:14.) God came to Abram in a vision and promised him a son twenty-five years before the birth of Isaac. (See Genesis 15:1–4.) Some of your dreams contain guidance about your future. If these dreams aren't recorded, you'll forget important details and maybe the dream itself!

Even if you don't think a dream is from God, write it down anyway. Many people do not think God gave them a certain dream because the dream made no sense. Many people have come to me with "nightmares" sent from the devil only to find out that their dream was from God after all.

Of course, God is not the author of nightmares. On the other hand, you may think a dream is a nightmare when it really is not. Just because it's very vivid or scary doesn't mean it's not God-given direction. It may be from God. It may not be. Here's a very important rule in receiving and learning to understand your dreams. *When in doubt, writer it out!*

After the dream "cools off" and you review it, it may make more sense to you. Date the dream when you record it. This can be very helpful later on as you look back on guidance you have received. The date can be very pertinent, perhaps even helping you put clues together to discern what God is saying. Ezekiel recognized the importance of knowing God's timing.

And it came to pass in the twelfth year, in the twelfth month, on the first day of the month, that the word of the LORD came to me. (Ezekiel 32:1)

Many Old Testament prophets knew exactly *when* God spoke to them. You should, too!

Let's review these simple steps to help you hear from God through dreams:

1. Ask God to speak to you in dreams.

2. Expect to receive.

3. When you wake up, be still for a moment and see if you can recall a dream.

4. Record *each* dream and date it.

Many times I'll wake up in the early morning hours and drift back into a light sleep. During these stages of drifting in and out of a lighter sleep, God often visits me with dreams.

Years ago, when I was just launching out in full-time ministry, I reached a place where I didn't know what to do next. I had quit my job. I had received numerous confirmations, yet no one was booking me for speaking engagements. I called out to God for help, and as I opened my Bible to seek Him, my eyes fell on a verse. *"I was watching in the night visions, and behold..."* (Daniel 7:13).

I sensed that God would speak to me that night in a vision! How exciting! I crawled into bed with expectancy. The next morning, as I was just beginning to wake up, I tried to recall a dream. I couldn't remember having a dream, however. Then, still in a state of being half asleep, I began to dream. I saw my pastor, and he said, "Proverbs 6:6–8." That was the entire dream. Needless to say, I got up and rushed to my Bible to find the passage.

Go to the ant, you sluggard! Consider her ways and be wise, which, having no captain, overseer or ruler, provides her supplies in the summer, and gathers her food in the harvest.
(Proverbs 6:6–8)

God told me to move in faith—don't just sit around and wait! I didn't know where to start, so I decided to call some pastors on Monday morning. At eight o'clock in the morning, I went to my office and prepared to make my first call. Before I picked up the telephone, it rang. A friend who was passing through town wanted to come by for coffee. I thought I was being sidetracked, but to be polite, I agreed to see him.

As we talked over coffee, I told him about wanting to call some pastors for some meetings. He gave me the names of some pastors he knew. After he left, I called the names he had given me. The pastors invited me to speak, and so I began my first full-time ministry tour!

That mini-dream proved to be very helpful in getting me started on the right track! Thank God! The dream came during a period of light sleep after I had begun to awaken.

Many times I wake up and don't remember dreaming at all. As I work at trying to remember a dream, one piece often drifts into my mind. As I think on that piece, another piece comes, then another. Finally, I put the entire dream together. These dreams often prove to be valuable sources of guidance to me. Other times, however, I could not recall all of the pieces from memory. In those cases, I just write down what I can remember and go on.

Receiving dreams from God is not too complex, is it? If you ask God to speak to you in dreams, He will! God has promised:

Call to Me, and I will answer you, and show you great and mighty things, which you do not know.   (Jeremiah 33:3)

As you follow the steps given in this chapter, you will *"dream dreams"*! (Joel 2:28; Acts 2:17.) Now that we've unlocked the gate into the world of dreams, let's step inside and broaden our knowledge of this land.

5

INTERPRETING DREAMS

So you awoke in the night and you had a dream!

Now what do you do?

Obviously, the next step is to interpret the dream so you can understand it.

When Jesus taught the multitudes and His disciples, He often spoke in parables. The parables had to be interpreted. God often spoke to the prophets using a similar pattern. He showed them a vision or dream and then gave them the interpretation. The vision was symbolic, and the symbols had to be interpreted to be understood.

Dreams follow the same pattern. You receive a dream. The dream contains symbols. The symbols must be interpreted. It's so simple! God has always used simple means to speak to His people.

Show and Tell

Remember the elementary school learning activity, "Show and Tell"? You brought in a craft or a favorite toy, displayed it before the class, and described it to them. God uses this same pattern to communicate to His people. God shows you something, then He tells you what it means. When you receive a dream from God, you must also search for the interpretation.

People tell me that they received a dream and the events occurred exactly as they dreamed it. Literal dreams can happen on certain occasions. They have never happened to me, however. The Scriptures contain no record of such dreams.

The Bible records dreams in which an angel sometimes appeared with a literal message. Dreams with a series of events, a plot, or even a simple message, however, always required interpretation in the Scriptures.

You must understand this concept to keep from being misled. The dream and its content often seem so real that you miss the symbolic meaning. Too often believers rely upon their own understanding rather than asking God for insight into the symbolic meaning of dreams.

Relying on natural thinking causes uninstructed Christians to veer off course when trying to understand a dream. You *must* learn to think symbolically! Let's look at an example from Scripture.

Then it came to pass, at the end of two full years, that Pharaoh had a dream; and behold, he stood by the river. Suddenly there came up out of the river seven cows, fine looking and fat; and they fed in the meadow.   (Genesis 41:1–2)

If a ranch owner had this dream today, he would probably think the dream involved his cattle. A subsequent verse reveals the real meaning of the cattle. *"The seven good cows are seven years"* (Genesis 41:26). Each cow symbolized a year. Interpreting that dream literally would cause a person to miss God.

Earlier in my ministry, I often traveled to my speaking engagements in a motor home. One night I dreamed I was driving the motor home when I encountered a very sharp curve in the road. Because I was traveling too fast, I barreled off the road. A literal interpretation of the dream would warn me about driving too fast. As I prayed over the dream, however, the Lord showed me that the motor home represented my ministry. I had made some quick decisions involving the direction of my ministry. God told me to slow down and make changes gradually. As I thought symbolically, I understood the dream and received an accurate interpretation.

In order to benefit from a dream, you must receive *and* interpret the dream. Some dreams are simple; others are more complex. Like any puzzle you attempt to figure out, some dreams are more difficult to interpret than others.

Divide Up Your Dream

How can we interpret a dream? I've discovered several helpful methods to uncover the meaning of dreams. When God created the heavens and the earth, He divided the big job into smaller, one day tasks and worked on His project one step at a time.

> *In the beginning God created the heaven and the earth....Then God said, "Let there be light"; and there was light. And God saw the light, that it was good; and God divided the light from the darkness. God called the light Day, and the darkness He called Night. So the evening and the morning were* **the first day.** *Then God said, "Let there be a firmament in the midst of the waters, and let it divide the waters from the waters." Thus God made the firmament, and divided the waters which were under the firmament from the waters which were above the firmament; and it was so. And God called the firmament Heaven. So the evening and the morning were* **the second day.** (Genesis 1:1–8, emphasis added)

That's the way you accomplish any big task, isn't it? You divide the large task into smaller tasks and approach the smaller tasks one step at a time. It's like eating a pie. After cutting the pie into pieces, you eat each piece one bite at a time.

You can use the same principle to interpret dreams. Don't try to understand the whole dream unless it's very short and very simple. Instead, divide the dream into smaller parts and work on understanding one part at a time. Let's look at how a dream should be broken up to approach it for understanding.

First, some dreams come in easily divisible sections. Often a dream may have two or three major parts or sections. These parts are like a play with Act I, Act II, and Act III. How do you know when a dream changes sections? The setting, the environment, or the action will change. This is difficult to explain, but it won't be difficult to spot once you examine a dream. The sections should be fairly obvious.

Here are two basic principles in interpreting your dreams:

1. Divide the dream into sections.

2. Divide each section of the dream into small pieces.

You shouldn't try to eat a whole piece of pie in one bite. In the same way, you shouldn't try to interpret a whole dream or whole section without taking little bites. Let's look at a passage of Scripture that illustrates this principle.

The angel who talked with me came back and wakened me, as a man who is wakened out of his sleep. And he said to me, "What do you see?" So I said, "I am looking, and there is a lampstand of solid gold with a bowl on top of it, and on the stand seven lamps with seven pipes to the seven lamps. Two olive trees are by it, one at the right of the bowl and the other at its left." (Zechariah 4:1–3)

In Zechariah's account of this night vision, he carefully described each piece in detail. Every piece was important. Even though he precisely described what he saw, he didn't understand the symbols. Don't grow discouraged if you're puzzled by the symbols in your dream. Each piece is there for a reason. Isolate each piece to find its meaning. By understanding the small pieces, you will receive interpretation of the entire dream.

Once a dream is divided into pieces, we must understand the meaning of each piece. Three methods of interpretation will help you to understand each individual piece and the dream in its entirety.

1. Ask God to tell you what each piece means.

2. Ask yourself questions about each piece of the dream.

3. Relate the dream to your circumstances.

Let's look at each method separately, using Scripture and personal experiences to illustrate how they work.

Ask God What Each Piece Means

The best way to receive an interpretation for your dream is to spend some time "getting in the Spirit" first. Many Christians do not know what it means to get in the Spirit. All believers can learn to do this, however, and it is scriptural. Jesus' disciples did this before receiving tremendous revelation from God.

> I was **in the Spirit** on the Lord's Day, and I heard behind me a loud voice, as of a trumpet.
> (Revelation 1:10, emphasis added)

> Peter went up on the housetop to pray, about the sixth hour. Then he became very hungry and wanted to eat; but while they

*made ready, he **fell into a trance** and saw heaven opened.*
(Acts 10:9–11, emphasis added)

One of the best ways to get in the Spirit is to use your prayer language or pray in tongues. Free your mind from the distractions and clutter of the day and focus it on God. We must be good listeners to hear the faint impressions of the Holy Spirit. We must cultivate the ability to quiet ourselves and listen. God's small, still voice is exactly that—it is small and it is still.

Once you have a hearing heart, pray over each piece of the dream. Ask God what the piece could mean. After you ask, listen for thoughts or for impressions. This is exactly what Zechariah did.

"What are these two olive trees, one at the right of the lampstand and the other at its left?" And I further answered and said to him, "What are these two olive branches that drip into the receptacles of the two gold pipes from which the golden oil drains?" Then he answered me and said, "Do you not know what these are?" And I said, "No, my lord." So he said, "These are the two anointed ones, who stand beside the Lord of the whole earth." (Zechariah 4:11–14)

If you don't understand your dreams, don't be afraid to ask God questions. Like Zechariah, your curiosity will be rewarded with answers Remember that God likes a seeker.

Like any skilled craftsman or artist, you need to practice to become skillful at dream interpretation. Don't be discouraged if you don't reap dramatic results immediately. Keep working with it. The skill and corresponding results will develop over a period of time.

Be sure to exercise discernment when using this method of interpretation so you won't be led astray. Remember the apostle Paul's advice: *"Test all things; hold fast what is good"* (1 Thessalonians 5:21). He also told the Corinthian church, *"By the mouth of two or three witnesses every word shall be established"* (2 Corinthians 13:1). Ask God to confirm in other ways that you're hearing from Him.

One morning I experienced a very vivid dream. I was in a large house with a friend and his mother. My friend was pacing the floor, wringing his hands. A giant stood in the front yard and yelled to my friend, "Come on out and fight! Come on out and fight!"

I remember thinking, He can't fight that giant. He will get beat up if he tries. That man is too big for my friend to fight. Then I turned to my friend's mother and told her, "You had better pray. He's thinking about fighting that giant."

Then I began to wake up. Before I completely awakened, I quickly asked God, "Was that really my friend?"

An answer came to me, "Uh-huh." I thought God might use King James English such as "Yea," or at least "Yes," but He used "Uh-huh."

Realizing that I was gradually waking up, I quickly asked, "Who was that giant?"

"Spirit of alcohol," the Holy Spirit said.

Then I was awake. I had been in the Spirit enough to get the interpretation. I've had the same experience during deep prayer. How did I know I heard correctly? That's a good question. After seeking the Lord, I decided it wouldn't hurt to ask my friend's mother to pray for him.

A few days later, my friend just happened to call. During the phone conversation I cautiously asked, "Have you been having some sort of a battle against alcohol?" As soon as I asked, he began to weep. These experiences confirm that you're really hearing from God.

My friend confided that he had been drinking twice that week—something he hadn't done in years. He had been going through a very difficult ordeal in his life, and under the pressure he had weakened and returned to an old habit.

"How did you know?" he asked.

"God told me," I replied.

"He did?"

"Yes."

My friend was shocked that God had released some information on his personal life. I reminded him of God's power to deliver, and then we prayed. When I saw him a few weeks later, he had not touched a drop of alcohol since our conversation. I believe that the victory was won through his mother's prayers.

Praying and listening is one way to interpret your dreams. If you don't get results this way, don't worry. You can still use methods two and three. Let's look at method two.

Ask Yourself Questions

The second method involves studying each piece of the dream and asking yourself questions about it. Examine your dream from every angle. You'll frequently receive revelation from God this way. In the same way that you receive nourishment from eating food, you must bite off a small piece of the dream and meditate on it until your spirit digests it.

Meditation on God's Word is the key to prospering in all that we do. God gave Joshua some very explicit instructions before he led thee Israelites into Canaan.

This Book of the Law shall not depart from your mouth, but you shall meditate on it day and night, that you may observe to

do according to all that is written in it. For then you will make
your way prosperous, and then you will have good success.
(Joshua 1:8)

Daniel knew how to ponder the pieces of a dream until God revealed the meaning. King Nebuchadnezzar received a dream and sought its interpretation. Dismayed that his own wise men and magicians could not understand it, he asked Daniel to declare its interpretation. When Nebuchadnezzar shared the dream. how did Daniel react?

Then Daniel, whose name was Belteshazzar, **was** [**aston-ished**] *for one hour, and his thoughts troubled him.*
(Daniel 4:19 KJV, empahsis added)

After pondering the dream for an hour, Daniel finally arrived at an interpretation. He was astonished for one hour. Synonyms for astonished include confounded, puzzled, perplexed, dumbfounded, and mystified. Daniel didn't understand the dream immediately. Scripture describes Daniel's unusual gifts or skills in the following passage:

Forasmuch as an excellent spirit, and knowledge, and under-
standing, interpreting of dreams, and shewing of hard sen-
tences, and dissolving of doubts, were found in...Daniel,
whom the king named Belteshazzar: now let Daniel be called,
and he will shew the interpretation.   (Daniel 5:12 KJV)

Let's briefly examine the term *"dissolving of doubts."* Sometimes revelation comes in exactly this manner over a period of time.

When I was a little boy, sugar used to come in cubes. My mother and the woman next door frequently enjoyed a cup of coffee or tea together. I often sat with them and watched their sugar cubes dissolve. When Mom dropped the cubes into two steaming cups of tea, I couldn't notice any change at first. Then, as Mom stirred her tea, the sugar cubes gradually got smaller and smaller. In a few minutes they dissolved completely.

That's exactly how revelation comes. Study a piece of a dream or ponder the meaning of a symbol. Think, probe, and meditate on it continually. As you examine it from every angle, the mystery of its meaning gradually dissolves. Finally, your understanding becomes clear and complete. Experience increases your ability to receive revelation in this manner.

As you study and ponder each piece, be like a good newspaper reporter. Begin to ask yourself the following questions:

1. Why is that piece in the dream?
2. What could it stand for?
3. If I think of this piece as a symbol, what would it be associated with?
4. Where did the dream occur?
5. Why did I behave that way?

As you use this method to review your recorded dreams, you'll begin to understand what God is saying to you. Remember Solomon's wise words: *"It is the glory of God to conceal a matter, but the glory of kings is to search out a matter"* (Proverbs 25: 2).

Method two, studying and meditating on the pieces of your dream, can help you receive all or part of the interpretation! Even after exhausting these first two methods, you can still use another resource that often unlocks the mystery to your dream. Let's look at this third avenue to revelation.

Relate the Dream to Your Life

You may not receive revelation using the first two methods. If so, review the dream and relate it to your life. Consider the other ways that God is speaking to you. One of Jesus' disciples used this method to unravel a puzzling vision that came to him during prayer.

> [Peter] *saw heaven opened and an object like a great sheet bound at the four corners, descending to him and let down to the earth. In it were all kinds of four-footed animals of the earth, wild beasts, creeping things, and birds of the air. And a voice* [said], *"Rise, Peter; kill and eat." But Peter said, "Not so, Lord! For I have never eaten anything common or unclean." And a voice spoke to him again the second time, "What God has cleansed you must not call common. This was done three times. And the object was taken up into heaven again. Now while Peter wondered within himself what this vision which he had seen meant, behold, the men who had been sent from Cornelius had made inquiry for Simon's house, and stood before the gate.* (Acts 10:11–17)

The last verse shows that Peter didn't understand the vision when he first received it. His revelation came as he watched a sequence of events unfold after the vision. The Holy Spirit gave him explicit directions:

> *While Peter thought about the vision, the Spirit said to him, "Behold, three men are seeking you. Arise therefore, go down and go with them, doubting nothing; for I have sent them."*
> (Acts 10:19–20)

Peter discovered these men were sent by Cornelius, a God-fearing Gentile. Peter and some brethren accompanied them to Caesarea to share the Gospel with all who assembled in Cornelius' home. Before Peter arrived, however, the meaning of the vision became clear.

> *Then he* [Peter] *said to them, "You know how unlawful it is for a Jewish man to keep company with or go to one of another*

nation. But God has shown me that I should not call any man common or unclean." (Acts 10:28, emphasis added)

Before he even finished preaching, many Gentiles believed. The gift of the Holy Spirit was poured out upon all who heard his words, which astonished the Jews who had accompanied him. Peter could only ask, *"Can anyone forbid water, that these should not be baptized who have received the Holy Spirit just as we have?"* (Acts 10:47).

At first, Peter didn't understand the vision. As events unfolded during the next three days, however, the vision made sense to Peter. His vision related to the events that followed it. By observing these events and putting all the pieces together, Peter got the revelation!

A few years after stepping into full-time ministry, I dreamed about driving my car down the highway. As I traveled along, I noticed the car in front of me turn onto another highway. I felt impressed to follow him, so I turned, too. Then, after he had gone a little way, he turned into a driveway. Again, I felt impressed to follow him, so I turned in, too. He stopped his car and got out. I stopped my car and got out. As I got out, I noticed a small school building. People gathered around the front door of this new school for a grand opening ceremony. As I observed them, I thought that God wanted me to open a school.

Daniel may have been astonished for one hour and Peter may have wondered what his vision meant, but neither of them had anything on me. I had no idea what that dream could possibly mean. Was I supposed to open a school? How could that possibly be? I traveled frequently in the ministry. How could I run a school? I followed the same advice that I've given you. I simply wrote the dream down, dated it, and went on with life as usual.

My wife and I were members of a church that operated a Christian school. Our two daughters were students in the school.

About two weeks after I had the dream, the pastor made a surprise announcement during the Sunday morning service. He said, "Please pray about our Christian school. We're not sure we're going to re-open in the fall. Every time we pray about it, God seems to give us a 'No.' "

Even after the pastor announced this, I never connected it with the dream. Another week passed. As a friend and I drove down a highway the following Saturday, I recalled the dream. Suddenly, I realized that the dream fit the circumstances. We were to take over the school and operate it! I felt sure God was speaking. When I returned home from the trip that evening, I said to my wife, "Guess what?"

She simply replied, "I know; we're to take the school." God had already spoken to her! Soon God directed me to buy some land and get a building. Then my wife had a dream in which our pastor backed a dump truck up to her and dumped all of the furnishings of the school—desks, books, everything.

As we prayed over that dream, the Lord seemed to say, "He's going to give the school to you—lock, stock, and barrel." When we approached our pastor and shared what we had been hearing from God, he gave us everything to run the school—the supplies, the books, the desks—even the checking account. The Lord led us to the land and the building. He also worked quickly so we could open by the fall. The school has operated successfully for over ten years.

When I first received the dream, I didn't understand it at all. This is very scriptural, as we can see from Peter's experience. Later, as events began to unfold, the interpretation became clear to me.

You'll understand a high percentage of your dreams by using this method. That's why it's important to review your dreams on a regular basis! I try to read through my composition book at least once each week. When reviewing, I usually go back as much as a month or two. Occasionally I go back six months or a year to review highlights. Glancing through my notebook, I can easily recognize a relevant dream. I just compare my entries with what I'm experiencing.

My dreams frequently reveal direction in several areas of my life, such as my ministry, finances, health, marriage, business, my personal relationship to God, and other pertinent areas of guidance. How do I keep track of all the guidance God gives me? Here's an organizational tip that frequently gives me additional revelation.

When I receive a dream that may apply to a specific area, I simply write "Ministry," "Health," or "Finances" next to the dream in the margin of my composition book. After receiving quite a few dreams, I record these general topics on the inside cover of the book. Then I number each page. Next, I go back to the topical headings and record the page numbers of pertinent dreams. This process helps tremendously whenever I want to review guidance on a particular subject. Revelation frequently comes to me when I review these "cold" dreams weeks or months after they occur.

Let's review these three methods of interpreting dreams. First, divide the dream into sections. Then divide each section of the dream into small pieces. Next, use the following methods to glean all you can from your dream:

1. Ask God to tell you what each piece means.

2. Ask yourself questions about each piece of the dream.

3. Relate the dream to yours circumstances.

"*Do not interpretations belong to God?*" (Genesis 40:8). Yes, they do. These three scriptural methods will help you glean interpretations from God so you can benefit from His guidance.

Spiritual truths are exciting, aren't they? To help you interpret your dreams, let's go to the next chapter where we'll discover some common symbols, the language of the Holy Spirit to communicate to us in dreams.

We've equipped ourselves with safety gear.

We've received the keys to unlock the main entry gate. We've taken orderly steps to travel in this new land.

As you explore the seemingly infinite new regions in this world, you'll be confronted with different boulders and odd-shaped barriers. You'll need to identify each one so you can properly negotiate the curves and forge ahead. A guide to these objects will be very helpful when you reach this stage of exploration. Such a guide is found in the next chapter.

Shall we proceed?

6

SYMBOLS—LANGUAGE OF DREAMS

We've taken a comprehensive tour of this vast land—the world of dreams. One more area still lies in front of us, however, before we conclude our tour. This is the area where symbols are found—and we will find all kinds of them.

God's use of symbols to communicate with man certainly won't surprise anyone who has read the Bible. The Old Testament prophets and patriarchs frequently heard from God this way. God gave them a vision or a picture of something, and then He revealed the meaning of the picture or symbol as the interpretation. Let's look at several examples:

Thus He showed me: Behold, the Lord stood on a wall made with a plumb line, with a plumb line in His hand. And the LORD said to me, "Amos, what do you see?" And I said, "A plumb line." Then the Lord said: "Behold, I am setting a plumb line in the midst of My people Israel; I will not pass by them anymore." (Amos 7:7–8)

Thus the Lord GOD showed me: Behold, a basket of summer fruit. And He said, "Amos, what do you see?" So I said, "A basket of summer fruit." Then the LORD *said to me: "The end has come upon My people Israel; I will not pass by them anymore."* (Amos 8:1–2)

Then I turned and raised my eyes, and saw there a flying scroll. And he said to me, "What do you see?" So I answered, "I see a flying scroll. Its length is twenty cubits and its width ten cubits." Then he said to me, "This is the curse that goes out over the face of the whole earth. 'Every thief shall be expelled,' according to what is on this side of the scroll; and 'Every perjurer shall be expelled,' according to what is on that side of it." (Zechariah 5:1–3)

Then Joseph said to Pharaoh, "The dreams of Pharaoh are one; God has shown Pharaoh what He is about to do. The seven good cows are seven years, and the seven good heads are seven years; the dreams are one." (Genesis 41:25–26)

You see the pattern, don't you? God gives a symbol followed by its interpretation. God chooses the symbol He wants to use, and we must seek Him for the interpretation of the symbol. Symbol and interpretation—it's not so complicated, is it?

When my daughters were in the first grade, they participated in "Show and Tell." Each student brought an object to school to show their classmates. While they displayed the object, they explained it to the other kids. Each child selected something different to show and talk about. One boy brought a pet hamster; another youngster brought his favorite toy. God uses this simple method of communicating to speak to us even today.

Remember this important principle: Show and tell is the symbolic language of your dreams. Jesus continually used this principle as He taught. When He explained faith, He illustrated His point by referring to mustard seeds, fig trees, and mountains. God still operates this way today. He hasn't changed.

Increasing Your Vocabulary

When I was a teenager, I spent a summer in Mexico with my aunt and two cousins. How strange it was to find myself in a new environment where most of the people spoke Spanish, a language totally unfamiliar to me. I had to learn a second language one word at a time. I often practiced association to learn new words at the dinner table. For example, when someone asked for the butter, I observed and listened. Gradually I associated butter with the word *montequilla*. I increased my vocabulary one word at a time until I could identify all the objects at the table with their corresponding names in Spanish.

The same thing happens when you first begin to understand the symbolic language of dreams. You must build your vocabulary one symbol at a time. Although you may receive a dream that is fairly simple to understand, many of your dreams may seem confusing. Don't be discouraged! The more perplexing ones get easier to interpret with time and experience. As your vocabulary of symbols increases, your ability to understand your dreams gets better and better.

While you ponder your dreams to learn the meanings of symbols, you'll need to consider one more factor. The Holy Spirit often uses a familiar symbol that you've seen in previous dreams. This makes the interpretation much easier to discern. Suppose, for example, that a lazy, lethargic person shows up in my dream. Then, after the dream, I struggle with a lack of motivation. I conclude that the dream had forewarned me about my coming struggle.

Let's suppose that a few months later I dream about this same person again. I dream that he's driving my car and I'm sitting in the passenger seat. Because of my earlier experiences, I have a good idea what this dream means.

1. I learned that my car often symbolizes my life.
2. I learned that particular person symbolizes laziness or lack of motivation.
3. That person is driving (or controlling) while I'm the passenger.

My vocabulary of symbols, developed by comparing my previous dreams to subsequent experiences, enables me to discern the interpretation of new dreams much more quickly. Teachability, time, and experience have developed my skill. My vocabulary is enlarging more and more, and I'm becoming increasingly fluent in the language of dreams. You can develop this same skill.

In the same way that you master a foreign language one word at a time, you must master the language of your dreams one symbol at a time. Every time you learn a new symbol and its corresponding meaning, you increase your ability to interpret dreams. Your skill gets better and better. You can improve it with diligence. You'll understand your dreams more quickly because you recognize symbols that repeatedly show up in your dreams.

Recognize Multiple Meanings

Interpreting dreams is not always as simple as we would like it to be. Sometimes symbols have multiple meanings. Perhaps the best way to explain this principle is through another example.

Years ago, when I was a young Christian, I dreamed about the pastor of my church. In the dream, I was in the passenger seat of a car and he was behind the wheel. As we drove down the highway, his face changed into the face of an old friend, then back into the pastor's face again. After I awoke and sought God about the interpretation, I remembered that my old friend was now a college professor. The Lord showed me that my pastor was going to be like a college professor to me. God would use this man to teach me about His ways. That turned out to be exactly what the dream meant.

In this dream, my old friend stood for his occupation. In an earlier dream that I shared with you, a man's old friend represented an alcohol problem. Every time you dream about an old friend, it doesn't mean the dream is about the friend's occupation.

People often misinterpret a dream this way. They assume that a symbol always represents the same thing every time it appears in a dream. God may use a symbol to stand for the same thing each time it shows up in your dreams. At other times, however, He may use a symbol to mean one thing one time, another the next. In the same way that some words have more than one meaning, some symbols have multiple meanings.

In other words, all symbols do not necessarily represent the same thing every time they're used. You can't simply refer to a list of symbols and their meanings and, presto, there's your interpretation! No!

We must give the Holy Spirit freedom to work. Seeking and finding is an important part of the process. Although interpreting some symbols will be repetitive, following God will always involve seeking and finding.

God's Use of Symbolism

Let's look at some examples in Scripture where the same symbolism is used in different ways. Jesus is referred to as the "*Lion of the tribe of Judah*" (Revelation 5:5). But the apostle Paul uses the same symbolism to refer to the devil. "*Your adversary the devil walks about like a roaring lion, seeking whom he may devour"* (1 Peter 5:8). Scripture also says, *"The righteous are bold as a lion"* (Proverbs 28:1). The Holy Spirit used the attributes of a lion to symbolize different things. Consequently, if you use a strict list of symbols to interpret your dreams, you may be disappointed or led astray. A list leaves no room for the Holy Spirit to be involved in the interpretation. Ask the Holy Spirit to give you insight. God may teach you a certain symbol and then use it repeatedly to convey the same meaning.

Suppose you have a dream about your daughter. What could God be saying?

1. God may be speaking to you about your daughter. Your daughter can stand for herself in a dream.

2. Your daughter may stand for something else. She may represent something in your life that is developing but is not complete or mature yet. She could be your ministry, your business, your health, your marriage, or a myriad of other things.

Beware of the person who always offers a quick, pat answer for the meaning of dreams. Those who blurt out instant interpretations are usually wrong in their conclusions. Beware of jumping to conclusions yourself with simple, easy answers to the symbols used by the Holy Spirit in a dream.

Although some dreams are easier to interpret than others, no one can receive quick interpretations to all dreams on the spot. Interpretations often require time, and they require seeking and finding. Remember the principle we discussed earlier?

*It is the glory of God to **conceal** a matter, but the glory of kings is to **search out** a matter.* (Proverbs 25:2, emphasis added)

As long as you're trying to hear from God in dreams and through other ways that He might speak, you'll find that this principle is true. Hearing from God always involves seeking and finding.

Let's cover a number of symbols that I've learned over the years. Reviewing them may help you solve some of the mysteries of your dreams. Don't use these symbols like a dictionary. Their meanings aren't locked in a preconceived definition or particular interpretation. They are simply guidelines that may give you some clues to the meaning of your dream.

Remember that some symbols will easily fit into previous patterns and lend themselves to easy interpretations. Don't lay down strict rules about symbols and their meanings. Allow the Holy Spirit to be involved. Let's look at some general symbols that may help you discover what God is saying to you in the night season.

Transportation

We've already discussed a few examples where vehicles showed up in dreams. The Holy Spirit often uses a car to represent your life. His variations are almost endless. For example, you may dream that you make a wrong turn while driving. This could warn you about making a wrong decision. A right turn could symbolize a right decision. A sweeping curve might mean gradual changes are ahead.

What other variations could God use? You may dream about getting a flat tire, going backwards instead of forwards, getting stuck in the mud, or driving off the main highway. You may be going too fast or too slow, or you may even find yourself in an accident. You may dream about someone else driving your car or someone giving you directions from the back seat. Even the type of car may hold significance. Were you driving a big car, compact car, truck, bus, or a foreign car? Do you see the endless possibilities? These variations could reveal things that are happening or about to happen in your life.

In the early years of my ministry, I traveled in a van to different churches. When I dreamed about that van, the dream usually referred to the ministry. Later, my family and I traveled in a motor home. Soon the motor home began to show up in my dreams. When I dreamed about the motor home, the dream usually gave me timely guidance about the ministry.

Later on in my ministry, I sold the motor home. I had two or three dreams that gave me some information about the transaction. In these dreams, the motor home actually stood for the motor home—not the ministry. Through prayer God enabled me to discern the difference.

Once I dreamed that I was riding in a jeep with my father-in-law. He drove up a very rough, steep mountain. Then we got out and walked to a beautiful, clear stream of water where I enjoyed a refreshing drink. In this dream, God (represented by my father-in-law) took me through some rugged terrain to bring me to a refreshing place in the Holy Spirit (the clear stream).

After praying about this particular dream, I found that my father-in-law represented God. You may discover that God will be represented by your father or father-in-law in your dreams, too. The next time I dreamed about my father-in-law, I had a hunch that he stood for God.

In this dream, we traveled in a jeep—a vehicle designed for rough terrain. The landscape and the vehicle foreshadowed that tough times were ahead. Sure enough, after that dream, God led me through some trials.

I gained comfort in knowing that my father-in-law was driving instead of me. Of course, that meant that he was in control. After encountering the rough terrain, I was refreshed with a drink from a cool mountain stream. I think that dream fits the experiences of many others who were led through rough places to find Jesus!

Boats can refer to a vessel for the Holy Spirit. If you dream you're traveling in a boat, the dream may be talking to you about your walk in the Holy Spirit. Again, God can use many variations. What kind of boat is in your dream—a row boat, a speed boat, a tug boat, or a yacht? Are you at the helm, or is someone else steering the ship? Are you moored to the dock, shooting the rapids, or drifting out to sea? Ask God to help you understand the various shades of meaning.

Once I dreamed I was in a boat going from Beaumont to Mexico. After having the dream, a pastor invited me to visit some missionaries in Mexico. That was the first of several trips I made. My dream about traveling there by boat simply meant I was being taken there by the Holy Spirit.

Water

Water may not always stand for the same thing. Once I dreamed about not being able to travel because water had flooded the road. In that dream, the water was not a type of the Holy Spirit but some circumstances that blocked me from my goal. When I encountered obstacles in my life, I broke through them to accomplish God's will.

You can even receive teaching in your dreams. A woman dreamed about a water-skier, a swimmer, and a scuba diver. While praying about the dream, she remembered the verse of Scripture about being cleansed with *"the washing of water by the word"* (Ephesians 5:26).

As she meditated on the dream, God showed her that some people are like the water-skier in relation to His Word. They hold the tow rope and say, "Go ahead, pastor! Pull me wherever you like." These people skim along the top of the Word, letting others do the work for them. They have only a superficial relationship with God.

The swimmer cut through the water with strong strokes. In the same way, some believers get into the Word and work at understanding it. The scuba diver, however, explored the very depths of the lake. Those who really meditate and study the Word of God discover a whole new realm that many people never experience. If you dream about water, ask the Holy Spirit to reveal its particular meaning.

House

Maybe you've been shopping for a house and then you dream about a house. Does this mean that the dream is about the house you're going to buy? Not necessarily. God may speak symbolically whether you're house hunting or not. Again, you must seek Him.

A house can stand for several things, including your life. If the house represents your life, the different rooms may have different meanings. The size, location, and decor of a room may contribute to the meaning that the Holy Spirit is trying to convey to you. Examine the upkeep of your house. Are the rooms cluttered, dirty, or in need of repair?

If you dream about the second floor or upstairs of a house, the dream may refer to your spiritual life. The bedroom sometimes refers to the intimate part of your life. Cracked cement block or a leaky basement may reveal trouble in the foundation of a person's life.

Believe it or not, even the bathroom of a house can convey meaning. I've dreamed about using the bathroom and eventually realized that the dream foretold about a purging experience God was about to take me through!

Every branch in Me that does not bear fruit He takes away;
and every branch that bears fruit He prunes, that it may bear
more fruit.   (John 15:2)

Does it seems strange that God would use going to the
bathroom to demonstrate a spiritual truth? If so, read the Old
Testament. God can be quite graphic.

People

Your friends, family, and co-workers frequently show up in
dreams. Although a dream about a particular person may be about
that person, the different characters in your dreams are usually
symbolic. God can use people to communicate a variety of things
in dreams. Among other things, they can represent:

1. Their position (banker, accountant, policeman, close
   friend, etc.)

2. Their personal attributes (lazy person, smart person,
   organized person, rich person, poor person, etc.)

3. Their name (they will have names with meanings in the
   dream)

4. Their age (mature person, little child, etc.)

5. Themselves (You dream about Aunt Sarah, and the dream
   really is about Aunt Sarah.) Be cautious here.

Aunt Sarah usually won't stand for Aunt Sarah. If you
dream about brothers, sisters, cousins, or nephews, the dream
could actually refer to the family of God. Sometimes your
brother may stand for Jesus. Your mother may stand for the
Holy Spirit. Your father or father-in-law may stand for God.
On other occasions, your brother or sister could stand for who
they really are!

People frequently represent their attributes. Your grandmother may stand for her steadfastness in the Lord, her love, or perhaps her old-fashioned ways. When Kenneth Copeland or Kenneth Hagin show up in my dreams, the Lord is speaking to me about my faith level.

Once a woman approached me after one of my meetings and asked for help with a dream. She began to relate her story to me.

"I dreamed I had a baby in my arms, and I was holding it toward my father. He wore a stern look on his face as if he disapproved. Only three days after the dream, my unmarried daughter had a baby. We had not known she was pregnant. It hadn't showed. What could the dream mean?"

I decided to ask a few probing questions. "What was your father like in real life?" I asked.

"Oh, he was very stern, harsh, and unforgiving. If I ever did anything wrong, he never forgot it and never forgave me," she replied.

"What was your reaction when your daughter presented you with her baby?"

"Why, I responded the same way my father would have. I was mad, and I didn't want to forgive her."

"Through the dream God put you in your daughter's shoes to remind you how it feels from her side," I told her.

"That must be right," she answered. "My husband kept telling me I needed to be more forgiving and tolerant. He was right."

In this particular dream, the woman's father stood for her father's attributes. In this case, the baby stood for a baby. The key to unlocking this dream was what the woman had experienced after having the dream. We were able to relate the dream to the experience.

God may even speak to you through the name of someone in your dream. While I sought God about how to schedule my speaking engagements, He visited me with a dream. The main character didn't really exist; God had created him just for the dream. His name was "Phil Monthly." Through his name, God instructed me to fill my monthly itinerary with speaking engagements during a certain season in my ministry.

Baby

As you begin to hear from God in dreams, you will probably dream about a baby. A baby can represent a lot of things. The Bible pictures young Christians as babies. *"As newborn babes, desire the pure milk of the word, that you may grow thereby"* (1 Peter 2:2).

A baby could also refer to something new in your life. The possibilities abound. If you dream you're expecting, don't buy maternity clothes until you have sought God for discernment. The dream could simply mean that something new is about to happen in your life.

In your dream a baby may not really be a baby. Even if you're a parent and you dream about your baby, the dream may or may not refer to your baby. The Holy Spirit can use babies, even your own baby, to mean different things at different times. A baby often symbolizes something in its early stages. Seek God for His interpretation. Learn to hear from Him in other ways, put the pieces together, and solve the puzzle.

Clothing, Jewelry, and Colors

The clothing you wear in a dream can certainly contain meaning. I have a certain sharp-looking sport jacket that makes me feel confident. When this particular coat shows up in my dreams, it's speaking of the same thing—wearing a positive self-image. Other clothes may represent your condition, spiritual or otherwise. Accessories such as a purse or billfold usually refer to your finances.

The shoes you're wearing in a dream can be a key symbol. Do your shoes fit? What kind of shoes are they—dress shoes, work shoes, or combat boots? What color are they? The shoes may represent your personal walk such as standards, behavior, etc.

Jewelry can have several meanings. Gaudy jewelry may reveal a woman's personality, behavior, or attitude. A wedding band may speak about your marriage. An earring may refer to hearing or listening. A wristwatch (or clock) may speak to you about God's timing.

Kathy dreamed about her older sister who was a Christian. In the dream Janice, normally a conservative dresser, wore expensive clothing. Kathy was shocked to see Janice wearing purple pumps, purple stockings, and a purple outfit.

"I couldn't believe you had spent so much money on a new wardrobe!" Kathy told her. "I tried finding those clothes everywhere, but no store carried them. Finally, I asked you where you had bought them. 'I went to a meeting at church, and they showed us how to dress this way,' you said."

In this case, the interpretation of Kathy's dream is pretty obvious. Janice wore expensive purple clothing—the color of royalty. The wardrobe, like the garment of salvation, couldn't be bought anywhere in the world. Janice got hers at church. God can speak to unbelievers in dreams, but it's usually about getting saved.

You may be aware of colors in your dream. God uses colors to convey certain meanings. Green often refers to life. Red can mean different things, including redemption or salvation. Isn't this appropriate since we're bought with the blood of Christ? Blue is sometimes used in conjunction with the Holy Spirit. White represents purity, holiness, or the presence of God. Orange may be a warning or danger.

Location

When trying to arrive at the interpretation of a dream, ask yourself, "Why did the dream take place where it did?" This question can produce tremendous insight about the meaning. The location of a dream usually has significance. For example, dreaming about being on a bridge may refer to a transition in your life.

Have you ever dreamed about the city, town, or house in which you were born? I was born in a small town in Louisiana called Hornbeck. Occasionally, I dream that I'm in Hornbeck. After dreaming about Hornbeck for several years, I finally realized its meaning. Why did some of my dreams take place there? Every time I dreamed about Hornbeck, the dream referred to something that was in the beginning stages. Hornbeck turned out to be quite an appropriate setting—it's where I began!

When Hornbeck shows up in my dreams, I realize that the dream refers to something in its beginning stages. I examine my life for the start of a new project or activity. Adding this new symbol to my vocabulary helps me understand future dreams that may incorporate that same symbol. Each time this happens, my ability to understand the Holy Spirit's language of symbols broadens.

If you dream you're in school or college, God may be talking to you about a learning experience. One night I dreamed I was in a classroom and was about to take a test. Sure enough, God forewarned me about a test in real life that I would be confronted with—not an academic test. If God tells you that a test is coming, hopefully you'll be prepared for it!

Your church could be a symbol for God's church, the body of Christ. Your church might represent your spiritual life. A dream about being in a hospital could either refer to God performing spiritual surgery or healing in your life. You'll find it exciting to study your dreams and get breakthroughs on the meanings of some of the symbols.

Sports

If you're an avid sports fan—and even if you're not—God can speak to you in sports terminology. Golf often shows up in my dreams, and it frequently gives me guidance about my life. If I'm using an eight or nine iron or a pitching wedge in the dream, it usually refers to my stage of completion of a project. Golfers use these clubs when they get close to the green. If I'm using a driver, the dream often refers to the starting point of a project. A putter can mean finishing up.

Examine different parts of your dream. The sport itself may hold great significance. Are you playing a team sport, or are you competing as an individual? Are you on the playing field or riding the bench? How much time is left in the contest? Are you the star in the championship series or the scapegoat for your team's loss? Look at your equipment and uniform for other clues.

Track has many interesting spiritual analogies. Are you clearing the hurdles? Did you fumble the baton on the relay team? Are you a sprinter or a long-distance runner? Are you running on a flat surface or cross-country? Ask God for insight as you dissect the different parts of your dream.

Smoking, Drinking, and Eating

When I dreamed about someone smoking a cigar, I nearly discounted it as having no spiritual value. After seeking God, however,

I realized that the cigar was a significant symbol. The person in the dream had drifted in his relationship with God, and the cares and influence of the world had begun to entice him. Smoking cigars and cigarettes or drinking alcohol often represents the spirit of the world.

Once I dreamed that I gulped a shot of whiskey before undertaking an endeavor. At first, I thought God had warned me about being influenced by the world. Through subsequent experiences, however, God showed me that taking a shot of whiskey stood for getting my courage up. Have you ever seen a movie where a gunslinger took a shot of whiskey for courage? The meaning was strictly symbolic. God didn't want me to drink whiskey!

One night I dreamed I was drinking catsup. Tempted to blame my strange dream on the pizza I had eaten the night before, I still asked God for insight. God simply told me that I was running behind schedule in some areas and needed to "catch up"!

Eating can be symbolic of feeding on the Word of God, especially if you dream about meat or bread. Fruit could refer to the fruit of the Spirit or bearing fruit. Eating cake may mean that some blessings are on the way. If you're eating poison, it might convey a warning about reading or listening to some unwholesome input or erroneous doctrine.

Eating can also symbolize communion, fellowship, or sharing with someone else. This fits Peter's vision in Acts 10 where God instructed him to eat unclean animals. Peter eventually understood the symbolism and began to fellowship with Gentiles. Had he taken the vision literally, Peter would have tried to find a restaurant that served pork chops when God wanted him to minister to the Gentiles.

Animals

Animals may show up in your dreams, and they have all kinds of possible meanings. Think about their primary characteristics.

Mules stubbornly resist their owners. Turtles withdraw into a shell and travel slowly. Beavers are industrious. Rabbits reproduce quickly. Where are these animals in your dream—roaming free, in a cage, or trapped?

Snakes, of course, can warn you about something evil. Scripture shows that a serpent is a type of the devil. (See Genesis 3.) Squirrels in my dreams often signify demon activity. This may also be true if you dream about spiders, scorpions, and other creatures.

Your own pet may show up in your dreams. God can speak to you about faithfulness, loyalty, and other things. Don't limit God. Ask Him to show you what He's saying.

A dove can be a type of the Holy Spirit. Remember Jesus' baptism? *"Then Jesus, when He had been baptized, came up immediately from the water; and behold, the heavens were opened to Him, and He saw the Spirit of God descending **like a dove** and alighting upon Him"* (Matthew 3:16, emphasis added).

Weather

You're probably all too familiar with the storms of life. Once I dreamed that a storm was coming. Some rough circumstances blew into my life, but I had been forewarned. God not only brought me through, but was nice enough to tell me in advance that trials were coming.

Some people may ask, "If you knew the storm was coming, why couldn't you pray it away or rebuke it like Jesus did?" That's a good question. Sometimes God warns us of a coming event so we can avoid the situation. God warned Joseph about Herod's order to kill all of the male children in Bethlehem. An angel appeared to Joseph in a dream and told him to flee to Egypt with Mary and Jesus.

The warning that Joseph received helped him avoid the coming danger. This was not the case of Joseph in the Old Testament, however. Although God warned Pharaoh of the coming famine, he still had to endure this hardship. Pharaoh wisely prepared for the food shortage his nation was about to face.

When God warns you of a storm or bad weather, He wants you to know what's going to happen. Then you can walk through the storm without being harmed. Again, one cannot take the simple route and come up with a pat rule. Each situation is different. God may warn you of a storm so you can command it to move like Jesus did. We must allow the Holy Spirit to be personally involved in dream interpretation and how we should respond.

God can use other weather forecasts besides stormy weather to speak to you. You may go through a cold place or a dry place that parallels your spiritual condition. A dark cloud may warn you of circumstances that could lead to depression. God can use weather and weather forecasting to talk to us in a variety of ways. I prefer to dream about blue skies and sunshine, don't you?

Music and Songs

Sometimes music stands for music, and sometimes it stands for other things. Once I dreamed I was singing in harmony with a man and his wife. Our voices harmonized together beautifully. At first, I thought the dream meant we would actually sing together. That never happened, but God built a strong relationship between us. This couple and I get along great, flow together, and work well together. Singing in harmony represented being in harmony with each other.

Sometimes when I first awaken from a dream, I hear a line from a song. Every time this has happened to me, the words were a key factor in the interpretation of the dream. The song does not have to be a spiritual song, either. I have usually heard the song before, and I'm familiar with it. Somehow God sifts through the thousands of songs that I've heard in my lifetime and selects the perfect line to fit the dream, conveying a big clue about the interpretation.

How does God do this? I don't know. It doesn't happen all the time. But when it does happen, it helps me to interpret the dream. Thoughts can go through your mind and you may not even be aware of them. Listen carefully to detect the faint promptings of the Holy Spirit. They are often present, but we must listen for them.

Other Symbols

Once I dreamed that I walked down a long flight of steps and then walked back up the steps. Like a lot of my dreams, I didn't understand the meaning of the steps until I went through some experiences that fit the dream. These steps represented the preparation I needed to handle a job God wanted to give me. The descending steps symbolized negative experiences I would encounter. The ascending steps were solutions I developed to handle these problems or to prevent their recurrence. I believe that God's school of management always includes some steps. These steps eventually equip you to handle the job with skill.

Hair can have some interesting meanings in your dreams. In the Old Testament, Samson's hair represented his anointing of strength and power. (See Judges 16.) In the New Testament, hair can represent a person's spiritual covering. (See 1 Corinthians 11:15.)

Hair can also have other meanings in dreams. Once I dreamed about the daughter of a minister friend of mine. In the dream, his daughter sported a very professional hairstyle, such as you might see on a woman with a business career. As I prayed, I felt that the dream really was about this man's daughter. I called my friend and related the dream. Sure enough, it fit. His daughter had been praying about enrolling in a business college to study for a professional career. The dream, along with other incidents, confirmed God's direction for her life. Getting her hair styled symbolized her preparation for a professional career.

Your teeth can refer to your words. If you dream about having dental problems, the dream may reveal your tendency to say the wrong things. Examine yourself and see if you need to guard your conversation against murmuring, gossiping, or complaining.

A key can symbolize a key principle or a key factor in a situation. It may represent the key to the solution. Soldiers, armies, and war obviously refer to spiritual warfare or being in a battle.

I haven't shown you every symbol that exists in the world of dreams. They are far too numerous. Even if I could show you every one, I wouldn't do it anyway. Now that you've received enough instruction to safely negotiate in and out of this land, it wouldn't be right for me to do more. I would rob you of the joy of your own discoveries as you pursue God's adventures in the night season.

A few more brief instructions might be in order before you and I say goodbye. Then I believe you'll be ready to travel this world on your own. I also want to answer any questions that you might have. Let's proceed towards the main entrance as we talk, shall we?

7

PUTTING IT
ALL TOGETHER

We've discussed safeguards, methods of interpretation, and symbolism in the world of dreams. Now you have all the necessary equipment for your own expeditions. But before you embark on your initial journey, let's walk through some of my previous dreams.

In this chapter I'll excerpt several dreams from the composition books that I've kept over the years. I'll describe the dreams exactly as I received them, changing only the names of individuals. I'll also share what was going on in my life when the dreams came. You'll see how I put all these principles together to arrive at accurate interpretations. I've gleaned some very timely, profitable guidance through God-given dreams. By following the examples in this chapter, you'll benefit from your own journeys into the world of dreams.

Recognize God 's Timing

God often gives me a dream when I'm very troubled over a particular situation. As a matter of fact, this is an important key. Many times God will visit you with dreams that address the very problems you're facing. This happened to Joseph, the earthly father of Jesus.

Now the birth of Jesus Christ was as follows: After His mother Mary was betrothed to Joseph, before they came together, she was found with child of the Holy Spirit. Then Joseph her husband, being a just man, and not wanting to make her a public example, was minded to put her away secretly. But while **he thought about these things,** *behold, an angel of the Lord appeared to him in a dream, saying, "Joseph, son of David, do not be afraid to take to you Mary your wife, for that which is conceived in her is of the Holy Spirit."*

(Matthew 1:18–20, emphasis added)

God visited Joseph with the dream at the time he was troubled over Mary's pregnancy. God often sends dreams when you're struggling with a problem. Timing may be a clue to God's purpose in sending you the dream. Expect God to give you counsel and guidance about a situation that's troubling you.

At the time of this particular dream, my gospel singing trio was preparing to record an album. Many months had passed since we had made our previous album. We had rehearsed the songs. The money had come in to cover the production costs. Everything was ready to go.

I was reluctant, however, to invest the money on this album. One of the vocalists in our group was having some personal problems in her walk with the Lord. Because of her spiritual condition, questions and doubts bombarded my mind. What if we made the album and then the trio broke up? Even if this singer left right after we made the album and we found a replacement, our new trio wouldn't match the photo on the album cover. Should I try to find a replacement for this vocalist before making the album? I really needed to hear from God on this decision.

My Dream and Its Interpretation

Just like Joseph, as I thought on these things, a message came to me in a dream. Here's exactly how it happened. I woke up about 2:30 AM, but couldn't recall a dream. Frustrated at waking up, I knew that I probably wouldn't be able to go right back to sleep. Sure enough, I tossed and turned for an hour or two. When I finally dozed off, it was into a much lighter sleep than my earlier, deeper sleep. As so often happens during this lighter sleep, a dream floated into my mind. I awakened immediately after receiving it. With a little effort, I recalled it and wrote down the pieces. Here's the exact entry in my composition book:

> Our trio is about to sing in an auditorium. Singer #1 and I are on the stage. All of the microphones and equipment are set up, ready to go. Singer #2 is sitting nearby at a table. Her hair is in rollers. Her mother is standing behind her, fixing her hair. My mother and father are seated nearby at another table. They're both looking at me. My father has his arms crossed and is tapping his foot, as if to say, "I'm waiting for you to get going."

That's the dream, just as it occurred. Let's work on the interpretation. Since this dream contains only one section, we'll simply break it down into pieces and study each piece.

Here's the first piece: *Our trio is about to sing.* We were in a preparation period before the actual activity. I feel that the trio is not symbolic. After praying, I sense that the dream is literally about our trio's music ministry.

Next piece: *Singer #1 and I are on the stage.* Why were we on the stage and singer #2 wasn't? Why weren't we in some other part of the room? This piece seems to say that #1 and I were ready, but #2 was not.

Next piece: *All of the microphones and equipment are set up.* As I think on this piece, I realize that the equipment being set up symbolized the circumstances in regard to our starting. All of the conditions are ready. The equipment is symbolic.

Next piece: *Singer #2 is sitting nearby at a table. Her hair is in rollers. Her mother is standing behind her, fixing her hair.* Why wasn't she on stage with us? Why was her mother fixing her hair? Why was it in rollers? This piece was easy for me. Her hair symbolized her spiritual walk or the condition of her life. She isn't ready like we are. Her mother is probably a type of the Holy Spirit, who is preparing her. The struggles in her life show me that the Holy Spirit is still getting her life in order. This piece fits what is really going on in her life.

Next piece: *My mother and father are seated nearby at another table.* I know from previous dreams that my mother and father often represent, respectively, the Holy Spirit and God (the Father).

The last piece contains the main message and purpose of the dream: *My father had his arms crossed and was tapping his foot as if to say, "I'm waiting for you to get going."* My father's actions show me that he's waiting for me to start.

Obviously, this dream instructed me to start moving toward the album rather than wait for singer #2 to get her life in order. God knew where she was right then. The Holy Spirit was preparing her. In the meantime, God wanted me to go ahead.

What was the result of the dream? I called the studio to schedule our album. God's hand seemed to be on the production of our new release. The album turned out fine. Singer #2 stayed with the trio for another two years. As God worked with her, she got her life in order. Although the circumstances looked shaky at that time, I was undergirded with the confidence that I was doing the right thing. I had heard from God!

Let's summarize the symbols in my dream. The trio in this dream really stood for the trio in real life. My father and mother were symbolic. Singer #2's mother was symbolic. The equipment being set up was symbolic. Singer #2's hair in curlers was symbolic. The dream fit what I was going through in my life right then. It was timely and very helpful.

Many times, guidance from God calls for action. Whether you hear from God in Scripture, prayer, godly counsel, or a dream, God probably wants you to do something with the direction He gives you. Scripture shows that this is often true.

> *But when Herod was dead, behold, an angel of the Lord appeared in a dream to Joseph in Egypt, saying, "Arise, take the young Child and His mother, and go to the land of Israel, for those who sought the young Child's life are dead." Then he arose, took the young Child and His mother, and came into the land of Israel.* (Matthew 2:19–21)

When you line up all the pieces and it looks like God is speaking, don't be afraid to act. Step out in faith, believing you have heard from God.

A Gem of an Opportunity

Several years later, I had another dream about making a record album. At this time I was singing and ministering on my own. I knew that it was time to make a new album, but I hadn't done much about it. When I woke up on the last morning of a ministry tour to North Carolina, I recalled a short dream. Here's the entry from my journal:

> George Smith hands me a small cloth bag. I open it and pour out its contents. There are two large jewels and several very small jewels.

As usual, I prayed and pondered the pieces of this dream. What would George Smith stand for in the dream? As I thought about my relationship with George, I remembered that he occasionally gave timely, large gifts to the ministry. Why were the jewels in a cloth bag? That's how some people would carry loose jewels. Why were there two large and several small jewels? Perhaps someone would donate two large gifts to the ministry and some smaller ones, too. I wasn't sure of this interpretation, but it seemed to fit. Was George himself going to give the gifts to me? That wasn't likely. Experience had taught me that characters in dreams are usually symbolic.

Subsequent events began to fit the dream. The man who had produced my last two albums called me that same morning from Nashville, Tennessee. A record company had agreed to offer me two new albums to be made simultaneously on their label at their expense. At that time, I had been praying about my own recording expenses on my own label. The albums would include some of the previous songs I had written as well as some new ones. In addition, the record company would promote and distribute the albums at their expense. Any profit from albums that I sold personally would go to my ministry. The record company would send me a royalty check for the ones they sold.

As I prayed over the opportunity, God seemed to give me a green light. The two big jewels stood for the two albums. The little jewels were the other bonuses the company offered, such as advertising and distributing the records. The arrangement turned out to be a very lucrative one for me.

A Convenient Meeting

A few years ago, I hired a contractor to pour a concrete slab for a new building on our church property. The forms were in place, the beams were dug, and it was time to pour the concrete. As a matter of fact, if we didn't pour the concrete right away, the entire project could be jeopardized. Sudden rain storms along the gulf coast are very common, and a hard rain could easily wash out the beams.

Our construction project also ran into some unexpected expenses, depleting our budget. If I poured the concrete, I would be $3,500 short of covering expenses. I felt compelled to have the concrete poured even though I hadn't raised the funds. The night before the construction company poured the slab, I awoke briefly and then drifted back into a light sleep. When I awoke the second time, I probed my memory for a dream. A dream slowly surfaced. Here's the dream just as I wrote it down:

> I walked into a convenience store. When I got inside, I ran into a friend of mine, John Brown.

What a short dream! As I studied the dream, I asked myself questions. Why did we meet in a convenience store? What could the store stand for symbolically? Who did John Brown stand for? Himself? In real life he was an attorney who occasionally contributed to my ministry. He might stand for someone who would donate to the ministry. Maybe he symbolized the money that would cover the deficit on the slab project.

Since I wasn't sure what the dream meant, I simply wrote it down for future reference. Anyway, the big day was here. I got up, dressed, and left for the construction site. As the work began that morning, I continued to pray about the funds. Later that morning, I remembered a previously scheduled lunch engagement at a nearby restaurant. I left the construction site and drove to the restaurant to meet my party. This particular restaurant had a luncheon buffet, so after meeting this person, I walked to the buffet line and picked up a tray. Just as I stepped to the table, the attorney I had dreamed about the night before walked right up to me. He just happened to be eating there that day. Neither of us frequented this restaurant. The timing was incredible!

"How are things going in the ministry?" he asked.

"Just great. Today we're pouring the concrete slab for our new building."

"How are the finances of the ministry?"

"The finances have been good, except for this slab expense. We came out about $3,500 short. I had to go ahead and pour the concrete anyway or risk losing the progress we had made."

"Come see me at my office this afternoon," he replied. Then he turned and walked away.

When I went to his office, we visited briefly. Then he called the bank where he was a board member and asked them to prepare a $3,500 check. When I returned to the construction site that afternoon, I had the money in hand to cover our expenses!

As I looked back over the dream, I understood it better. The convenience store simply stood for a place of convenience. God arranged the perfect timing of our meeting. This divine appointment made it convenient for me to get the necessary funds for the project. In this dream, the man I ran into actually stood for himself. More often than not, however, a person is symbolic.

When I stepped up to the buffet line and saw him, I naturally remembered the dream from the night before. The dream suddenly fit my circumstances. God orchestrated the entire matter perfectly, then showed me in advance so I would recognize His timing and provision.

Ordering My Priorities

During a time when my schedule was unusually busy, I fell into a subtle trap. I began to neglect my devotional time with the Lord. I knew that I needed to pray and read the Word, but somehow I kept putting it off. God knew my schedule had sapped my spiritual strength, so He sent a dream to get my attention.

One night, I went to bed early and slept soundly until morning. As soon as I awoke, I tried to recall a dream. With a little effort, a fairly vivid dream came into my memory. Here's the dream as I wrote it down:

> I'm driving my car into a gas station to get some gas. There's snow on the ground. I stop the car, get out, and approach the two gasoline pumps. One is marked regular; the other is premium. The price of the regular gas is 79 cents per gallon. Then I look at the premium, and it is $1.29 per gallon.
>
> "A dollar twenty-nine!" I say. "I'm not about to pay that much for premium! I'll use regular." Then I began to fill up the tank with regular.

I wrote down the dream and dated it. During my prayer time that morning, I studied and prayed over each piece. As I looked at the first piece of the dream, I felt like the car represented my life. Then I asked myself, Why was there snow on the ground? As I prayed over this piece, it seemed that the snow meant I was in a cold place spiritually. That certainly seemed to fit.

Next, as I prayed over the two gas pumps, marked regular and premium, revelation drifted into my mind. Here's what the Lord seemed to say through my thoughts: You've been in a cold place lately. When you looked at the great difference in price between the regular spiritual walk and the premium walk, you decided to settle for the regular walk. You didn't want to pay the much greater price for the premium walk.

Wow! That dream was quite revealing! I decided not to be so busy in the future. I confessed my neglect of prayer and Bible study, asked God to forgive me, and pressed in to know Him in my devotional time. The dream really motivated me to get more serious about my time spent with God. As a result, God renewed my spirit and enabled me to serve out of the strength He supplies.

Getting in Shape

God used a dream more than once to adjust my priorities. At another time, my traveling schedule pushed me to my physical limit. After speaking in a different town each night, I drove long hours the following day to reach my next destination. Finally, my body began to hurt. I woke up each morning feeling tired. One morning I woke up and then drifted back into a light sleep. Upon waking up the second time, I realized I had experienced a fairly simple dream. Here's the entry in my composition book:

I'm in a doctor's office. The doctor tells me, "Slow down or speed up." As he said speed up, he pointed his finger toward the sky.

I didn't have to study or pray over this dream. God sent me a strong warning that I was endangering my health by pushing my body beyond its limits. If I didn't stop, it would actually shorten my life. Needless to say, I cut back my schedule. I wish all dreams were as easy to understand as this one!

God also dealt with me about not getting any physical exercise. Being so busy, I had taken no time to develop a personal exercise program. God wanted me to take care of my body and my spirit. He used an interesting series of events to get my attention.

One of the first grade students in our school at that time was a bright young boy named Jason. In the midst of these events, Jason showed up in one of my dreams. Upon awakening one morning, I probed my memory for a dream. In less than a minute, the pieces drifted into my mind.

I'm standing with Jason's father by Jason's desk in our school. Jason is seated at his desk. I said to the man, "Jason sure is a smart student. He always obeys his teacher and does what she says."

Jason's father looked at me and asked, "Is he smarter than you?"

This dream is not so complex. God showed me that even a first grader knew that he should obey his teacher. I certainly should know to obey my Teacher. The Bible says, *"But the Helper, the Holy Spirit, whom the Father will send in My name, He will teach you all things, and bring to your remembrance all things that I said to you"* (John 14:26).

Obviously I wasn't obeying the Holy Spirit in some area. I suspected it was in not initiating an exercise program. Soon God sent me a confirmation.

Our youngest daughter loved animals and always had a pet of some kind. At this time, she had a pet hamster. Just a day or two after my dream about Jason, I walked into the living room where we kept the hamster's cage. His exercise wheel spun wildly as he ran at full speed. When I reached in to pick him up, I noticed how his heart hammered away from the exercise. I called to my wife in the next room, "Honey, come feel the hamster. He's been running in his exercise wheel, and his heart is pounding."

As soon as I finished speaking, the Holy Spirit spoke to me. "Is he smarter than you?"

Not only was a first grader using more wisdom than me, but even a hamster knew he had to exercise! I started my exercise program that very day and have continued it ever since. If I'm tempted to slacken, I remember my dream about Jason and my experience with the hamster. Together they have probably added years to my life.

Guidance in Ministry

When our church was very young, I confronted many problems that most young pastors have. One situation in particular caused me a lot of concern. A married couple who operated in a spirit of rebellion caused problems in our church. I prayed earnestly about how to handle the situation. A dream came to me on the morning that I was to return home from a ministry trip. When I first awakened, I couldn't recall a dream. As I lay in bed for a few moments, the following dream drifted into my memory:

> I'm standing in the parking lot of our church. Two trees have fallen over. One is blocking the parking lot so cars can't get in. The other is covering up the sign so that it can't be seen. I get out my chain saw, cut up the trees, and haul them off.

I wasn't sure about the meaning of this dream, so I prayed over the pieces. Why did the dream take place in the parking lot? As I prayed over that piece, I realized that if the parking lot were blocked, then no one would come to our church. As I prayed about the sign being blocked, a similar thought came to me. If the sign is blocked, then no one would know the church was there. The more that I prayed, I realized that this dream related to the growth of my church being blocked. Something had blocked the growth of the church, and I got rid of whatever it was.

Then I prayed about the power saw. What did it represent? It stood for a tool that was powered to handle the job. What kind of tool could that be? During the next two or three days, I continued to pray over these clues. Finally, I felt sure that I had reached the right conclusion. This couple was blocking the growth of our church. I needed to use the power that God had given me to get the problem resolved.

I prayed the prayer of authority over the rebellious spirits that were operating through this couple. I also discussed the problem with them and took some corrective action to alleviate the situation. After two sessions with me, they decided to leave our church. As soon as they left, the atmosphere in our church changed. Just as the dream had shown me, new growth began to occur. This dream helped me make the right decision for the health of our church.

The following week I received another dream about church growth. Unlike the first dream, this one occurred in the middle of the night. Here's the entry from my book:

> My wife and I are in the church auditorium. She's putting out some extra folding chairs, one at a time. Seated in the sanctuary are four people. Each of them is a person we have ministered to at different times in our life.

I sensed that the dream referred to the church itself. My wife was putting out folding chairs one at a time. This told me that growth would come gradually. God would add to our numbers one by one. The growth would come as a result of ministering to those whom the Lord sent. In subsequent months, events proved this dream to very accurate. God brought new growth to us in the exact manner shown in the dream!

Important Decisions

Let me share one more story with you. This one occurred at a time when I faced a big decision—leaving full-time employment to go into full-time ministry. That's certainly a very big step. Reasoning and logic told me how foolish I was to leave the security of a salaried job to follow the Lord. Although I felt that God was leading me, uncertainty about the future tempted me to waver.

At the same time I was struggling with this, two friends of mine were leaving their salaried jobs to go into a business venture together. At the last minute, one man lost his nerve and backed out, choosing to stay with the security of his existing job. I learned about his decision on the very day that I was tempted to do the same thing.

That night I went to bed and slept soundly. The following morning, I probed my memory to see if God had spoken anything to me during the night. At first, I remembered only a fragment of a dream. As I meditated on it, the rest of the pieces came to me. Here's the dream as I wrote it:

> Jack (the friend who lost his nerve) is playing football. He runs out for a long pass. The quarterback throws the pass, and he catches it. He looks around. The field is wide open. Nobody is even near him. He has a wide open shot for the goal line and a touchdown. Fear grips him, however, and instead of running for the touchdown, he simply falls to the ground and covers the ball.

I knew that this was what was happening to my friend. As I prayed over the dream that morning, I knew that God was using my friend's situation to talk to me about my similar circumstances. I had caught the pass. The field was wide open for a touchdown. I got the message. Heeding the warning of the dream, I resigned my job and entered the ministry. Fear did not stop me from stepping out!

In this instance, the interpretation to the dream came to me during prayer. The dream was so short and fit my circumstances so clearly that I never divided the dream into pieces. Before I had a chance, the meaning just burst into my thoughts. The dream related to what I was going through in my life at that time—and it helped me to make the right decision.

I hope my experiences encourage you to visit the world of dreams again and again. You'll gain valuable experiences of your own in days to come. We're close to the gate where we originally began this exploratory journey. I want to answer any questions you might have. Let's pause for that now, shall we?

8

QUESTIONS
AND ANSWERS

Before we conclude our tour, I would like to answer some common questions about the world of dreams. Perhaps you're wondering about my earlier remarks and instructions. People who attend my seminar on how to hear the voice of God frequently ask numerous questions at the close of my meetings. These lively discussions often shed additional light on the study material. Perhaps if I review some of their most commonly asked questions, you'll find some issues that may have crossed your mind.

1. Do all dreams have meanings?

Not necessarily. When I'm very tired, I often lie down and began to dream almost as soon as I close my eyes. My mind meanders around, sort of dreaming, but with no theme or pattern. When you get into the flow of receiving dreams from God, however, you'll find that most of your dreams contain meaning. As this aspect of your relationship with God develops, you'll expect the Holy Spirit to be involved in your life in the night season. As you learn to flow in this, you'll find that many of your dreams contain anointed counsel from God.

2. Being a light sleeper, I find that my mind dreams constantly. If I recorded all these dreams, I would be writing all night. What do you suggest I do?

Your situation is very unusual, but I occasionally meet people who have this problem. Ask God to awaken you only after He gives you a dream so you can sleep through the night. I believe God can help even light sleepers to sleep more deeply.

3. Sometimes my dreams have sexual connotations. Surely these dreams don't come from God. What should I do?

The sexual drive is powerful and can influence our thoughts while we're asleep. Someone who struggles with lust may find their dream life affected by sexual thoughts sometimes. On the other hand, do not simply discount a sexual dream. God can use a sexual scenario to speak to you. Please exercise discernment in understanding these dreams.

The Song of Solomon certainly uses graphic sexual language to paint a picture of spiritual meaning. If a married person dreams about a sexual scene with his or her mate, the dream could simply be speaking about the couple's relationship but not necessarily their sexual relationship. In counseling people I've found that sexual dreams are often dismissed as not divinely inspired when they may hold significant meaning. Pray about the dream and ask God to open your understanding.

Obviously, God does not endorse immorality. He will not give you a dream to tell you to commit adultery or fornication, but He might give you a dream to warn you of it. Again, pray and use discernment.

4. I spent an entire day fishing. That night I dreamed I went fishing. Didn't I dream that simply because I

had spent the whole day doing that very thing?

Not necessarily. God often speaks to us through our activities and interests. Even though you were involved in doing something all day, don't rule out God's ability to speak to you through it. Remember, "When in doubt, write it out." Then review it, study it, and give God the opportunity to speak to you through your dream.

5. I don't ever have dreams. Do you think God will speak to me in a dream?

Yes, I do. As you follow the steps in this book, I believe you'll begin to recall your dreams and hear from God through them. Remember the admonition, *"You do not have because you do not ask"* (James 4:2). If you ask God to speak to you in the night season, He will do just that.

6. After listening to your teaching on hearing the voice of God, I recalled a few dreams. After a while, however, the dreams seemed to fizzle out. Why?

Usually this occurs when a person forgets to follow the steps given in chapter four of this book. If you try to recall your dreams immediately upon awakening, you probably will receive more dreams. Read that chapter again, follow the steps, and see if you get back into the flow of hearing from God in your dreams.

7. The Bible says, *"Your young men shall see visions, your old men shall dream dreams"* (Acts 2:17). I'm a young man. I guess I'm getting visions, not dreams. Can you explain why the Bible makes this distinction?

Dreams and visions are closely related. Dreams take place when we're asleep. Visions often occur when a person is awake or in prayer, but God also visited people with visions in the night. (See Daniel 2:19; Acts 18:9.)

On the day of Pentecost, Peter preached the fulfillment of Joel's prophecy. Scripture says, *"Your **old men** shall dream dreams"* (Acts 2:17, emphasis added). Dreams can be complex.

Spiritually speaking, you must be mature to flow in dream interpretation. Hearing from God in this way requires more maturity and discernment than other things of the Spirit.

Scripture refers to different levels of maturity in the body of Christ. Examine the stages of growth in the following passages:

> As **newborn babes**, desire the pure milk of the word, that you may grow thereby.   (1 Peter 2:2, emphasis added)

> **My little children**, these things I write to you, that you may not sin. And if anyone sins, we have an Advocate with the Father, Jesus Christ the righteous.
> (1 John 2:1, emphasis added)

> I have written to you, **young men**, because you are strong, and the word of God abides in you, and you have overcome the wicked one.   (1 John 2:14, emphasis added)

Dream interpretation is a skill that you must develop over a period of time. The truths in this book didn't come to me overnight. I've invested years in learning to hear from Him in this way. If you have a teachable spirit, you'll mature in hearing from God in the night season, too.

8. I used to be involved with the occult before I became a Christian. At that time, I delved into dreams and their interpretations. Wouldn't it be unwise for me to hear from God in this way because of my past experience?

Your concern is understandable. Remember that the occult is only a counterfeit of the genuine supernatural manifestations of the kingdom of God. The occult encourages its followers to meditate. That doesn't stop me from meditating on the Word of God. Occultists achieve a trance-like state to contact spiritual entities. That doesn't stop me from seeking God's presence through prayer. The occult endorses fortune telling and supernatural guidance. The kingdom of God manifests itself with powerful spiritual gifts such as the word of knowledge, the word of wisdom, and prophecy. (See 1 Corinthians 12.)

A born-again believer who consulted a fortune teller before coming to Christ should-n't fear offering himself to God as a vessel for spiritual gifts. Once you receive Jesus as your Lord, you should turn from the occult. Denounce any previous involvement with unclean spirits and command them to stop tormenting you. Ask God to cleanse you and forgive you for this sin. Bad past experiences don't have to rob you of the future blessings that God has stored up for you. If you follow these instructions and don't operate in the occult, you'll find the occult won't operate in you.

9. Can the devil give dreams?

I have a friend who became a Christian at a young age. As she grew older, she began to stray from the Lord. In ignorance she even experimented with the occult. Soon after this, she began to experience evil dreams. Involvement in the occult can open the door for demonic influence in one's life, including one's dream life. Once a person comes to Christ and begins to walk with God, these previous involvements lose their influence on a person. Of course, God will not torment you in a dream. As with any other means of hearing from God, use discernment.

Once I experienced a false vision as I was waking up. Its guidance didn't line up with the other direction God had given me. Not everything you receive is God-inspired. Remember what I've already said about recording your dreams so you can study and review them. Over time you'll know if God is speaking or not.

While not all dreams come from God, I've discovered that most people lack discernment and discard a dream too quickly because they don't understand its meaning. Don't be too hasty in dismissing those perplexing dreams. You may miss God. Once you get into God's flow, you'll find that most of your dreams are God-inspired.

10. I used to dream quite often, but I got discouraged in trying to understand my puzzling dreams. The dreams often seemed too complex to understand. Can you help me?

Continue to record your dreams and pray over their meanings. Time and patience are very important in developing your ability to understand the language of your dreams. If you seek God, He will show you that He's speaking to you. Don't forget that He's a rewarder of those who diligently seek Him. (See Hebrews 11:6.) Mix a seeking attitude with time and patience, and I believe you'll begin to experience more positive results.

11. Should I teach my young children to hear from God in this manner? Isn't this too confusing for a child?

Joseph was seventeen when he received a prophetic dream that made his brothers jealous. (See Genesis 37:2,5.) The Bible doesn't reveal if this was his first encounter with dreams or not. A teenager can hear from God in this manner. As a matter of fact, a child can receive God-inspired dreams, too. I've known it to happen.

Young children should never be discouraged if they ask a parent about their dreams. Listen attentively to your children and pray with them. My daughters sometimes shared their dreams with me. When they were younger, their dreams seemed to be the result of active imaginations. I tried to listen patiently and promised to pray over the dream for discernment. I didn't want to discourage them.

As they got older, my daughters began to receive some guidance about their lives through dreams from the Lord. I also remember a few instances when God definitely spoke to them even when they were eight or nine years old. I didn't encourage my children to write down their dreams until they reached their late teens. Use your own common sense and judgment as a parent. The Lord will lead you as to timing and so forth. If your child is tormented with nightmares, you can certainly pray and ask God to set him free.

12. What about deja vu, the feeling of knowing what's going to happen before it happens? Sometimes I've felt I I've actually lived through an experience by way of a dream or other foreknowing.

God can foretell events before they occur. The Bible repeatedly substantiates this fact. If God reveals advance information to you about something that's going to occur in your life, He will always have a reason for telling you. He may want to warn you, guide you, or assure you that He will bring you through a difficult situation.

As for a certain "feeling" of having been through a situation before the situation unfolds, I've never been able to pinpoint such a feeling as God-given guidance or not. God will not tell you about an event before it occurs just for the sake of telling you. If God tells you, He will have a reason for doing so. Seek Him and find the reason.

13. Aren't you afraid of what might happen when you teach people to seek guidance from dreams and visions? Won't some people fall into error and make bad decisions because they think they heard from God in a dream?

No, I'm not afraid, but I do realize that some people may misinterpret a dream and make a bad decision. Hearing from God in dreams involves some risk, but you can minimize the danger by following the safeguards in chapter three. I suppose God faced the same possibility when He wrote the Bible. Knowing some people would take scriptures out of context, He wrote it anyway. The concepts and principles presented in this book are tested and proven. I've done my best to present the truth with integrity and care.

If you make a mistake in hearing from God in dreams, learn from your experience. Did you act too hastily? Did you hear from God in other ways? Did you misinterpret the symbolism of your dream? If you have a teachable spirit, none of your experiences need to be wasted—and that includes mistakes.

14. I know a Christian woman who has a reputation for interpreting dreams for others. Several people I know are constantly going to her for guidance. Is that right?

No, it's not a good idea for these people to become dependent on her. When you continually go to another person to get your guidance from God, you're opening the door for that person to control your life. While I do help others to understand their dreams from time to time, I encourage them to pray and seek their guidance from God. Certainly people with experience of any kind can help others with less experience. It's not healthy, however, for another person to control you and the important decisions in your life. Relationships where a dominant person controls a weaker person border on witchcraft or fortune telling.

In order for you to develop in your relationship with God, you must spend time to hear from God and understand what He's saying to you. When you do need prayer or counseling, consult your pastor. Don't run to him or anyone else each time you have a dream, however. Run to God.

15. I dreamed I was ministering to thousands of people in a gospel meeting in Africa. Do you think God is calling me to be a missionary to that country?

Ask God to show you in other ways what He's saying. If you get confirming guidance, then cautiously pursue what you think He's saying to you. Constantly monitor new clues and check interim guidance as you move. If God is guiding you, He will prove that you're on the right track. God always works on both ends of a situation when He's involved.

I also encourage you to seek confirming counsel from your pastor. Scripture says, *"A man's gift makes room for him, and brings him before great men"* (Proverbs 18:16). If God has a call on your life for this work, other godly leaders will recognize the anointing in you. Your pastor can set you apart for that ministry in God's time and with God's resources. Remember that *"in the multitude of counselors there is safety"* (Proverbs 11:14).

16. I experienced a dream that was quite vivid. I wrote it down, prayed over it, reviewed it on several occasions, but never understood its meaning. What should I do?

You're doing the right things. When I receive a dream that still perplexes me after I've given it some prayer and time, I simply leave the dream alone. I don't believe that every dream is God-inspired.

17. I frequently receive dreams about other people. When I tell them about the dreams, they usually don't want to receive the advice I have for them. Should I keep trying to help other people this way?

Be very cautious about giving others advice from dreams (or other means of guidance). Many times people in your dreams are simply characters that God uses to speak to you about your own life. A counselor may receive guidance through a dream to help a counselee. This is an area where it is easy to misinterpret what God is saying, however. Use caution. Your natural mind can cause you to miss what God is really saying.

18. I dreamed I was riding a horse through a stream. In front of me was a beautiful field of grain, ready to harvest. Can you help me understand this dream?

Yes, I can. Take the tools given to you in this book and use them. Examine what is happening in your life. Ponder the parts of the dream. Seek God and His counsel. Did He give you the dream? What is He saying? God is able to help all who come to Him in faith. When people ask me about dream interpretation, I refer most of them directly to God for the answer.

I receive other questions from time to time, but I think we've covered most of them in other sections of this book. We're almost back to our point of origin now. Let's pause for my last brief instructional session, shall we?

9

IT'S UP TO YOU!

Finally, we're concluding our tour! Now you know enough about this land to come and go on your own. I've shared what God has shown me about hearing from Him in dreams. What you do with this knowledge is up to you.

The world of dreams is a good land. Subsequent journeys into its vast territory can benefit you in many ways. I'm convinced that God has given this land to end-time Christians to possess. I hope you'll enjoy many more visits here in days to come.

One final instructional session is in order, however, before we part. As I share it with you, why don't you reflect on this vast land that we've explored together? As you consider the challenging terrain that we've traveled, please realize an important truth.

Different people have different experiences after taking this tour. Some people grasp these teachings and begin to hear from God in dreams immediately. Their success doesn't seem to be long lived, however. Their interest wanes, they lose their hunger to hear from God, or they become too busy to record their dreams. Others hear the message, begin to operate in the principles, and continue to hear from God in the night season on a consistent basis. As they grow and learn, they reap immense benefits from receiving and interpreting God-given dreams.

Some people never discipline themselves to recall a dream when they wake up. "I just don't remember my dreams," they lament. What's the difference between those who remember their dreams and those who don't? Those who cultivate a sensitivity to the Holy Spirit as they gradually wake up usually remember their dreams. Many of their dreams are inspired guidance from God. If they don't write these dreams down, however, they forget important details that are crucial to the interpretation.

Others try to recall a dream each time they awaken. They diligently record each dream and date it. They review these dreams often, looking back over the dreams they had last week, last month, or even several months ago. These people have discovered divine guidance coming to them in the night season. They're developing their skill to understand what God is saying to them. They know that it's real. They know that it works. And it's producing rich dividends in their lives.

Reaping the Benefits

Jesus often used parables to teach spiritual truths. The parable of the sower is one of the few parables in which Jesus actually gave the interpretation to His disciples. Let's look at His discourse and its interpretation:

The sower sows the word. And these are the ones by the wayside where the word is sown. And when they hear, Satan comes immediately and takes away the word that was sown in their hearts. These likewise are the ones sown on stony ground who, when they hear the word, immediately receive it with gladness; and they have no root in themselves, and so endure only for a time. Afterward, when tribulation or persecution arises for the word's sake, immediately they stumble. Now these are the ones sown among thorns; they are the ones who hear the word, and the cares of this world, the deceitfulness of riches, and the desires for other things entering in choke the word, and it becomes unfruitful. But these are the ones sown on good ground, those who hear the word, accept it, and bear fruit: some thirtyfold, some sixty, and some a hundred.

(Mark 4:14–20)

One day I was cleaning some cluttered drawers at home when I found an old membership roster of a church my wife and I had attended as young Christians. As I thumbed through the roster, the truth of this parable dawned on me. Many of the people on the list had fallen prey to the pitfalls that Jesus described.

After enjoying a glorious experience with the Lord, some immediately turned their back on Christ and returned to their old way of life. Others endured for a time, but when they encountered afflictions and persecutions, they deserted the faith. Some who were very excited about Jesus slowly faded back into the lures of the world. As Jesus foretold in this parable, however, some remained active, faithful disciples who bore good fruit in their lives. And some experienced greater fruitfulness than others.

These same principles apply to those who hear teaching on receiving dreams. Many embrace these truths with excitement, especially after God speaks to them in the night season. Some drift from the teachings and stop receiving dreams for a variety of reasons. Some continue for a season in recalling, recording, and praying over their dreams, but eventually they stop receiving dreams from God. Some persist even longer, but eventually they get discouraged because of the effort. Many stop seeking God in the night season.

Others, however, record and study their dreams on a consistent basis. They pray over them and seek God for the interpretation. They benefit greatly from God's guidance through their dreams.

Recalling Your Dreams

I occasionally get to follow up on people who have heard my seminar. I'm always curious to know if they're applying these principles to their lives. While preparing my message for an evening service at a church, my mind drifted to a conversation with the pastor earlier that afternoon.

"How did you happen to schedule me to preach in your church?" I asked.

"I ordered your teaching series on hearing the voice of God and enjoyed the tapes, so I decided to contact you about coming here for some meetings."

"Oh, you've listened to my series on the voice of God?"

"Yes."

Here was my chance to find out about the effectiveness of the course. I asked him a pertinent question.

"Have you been hearing from God in dreams?"

"Occasionally I get a dream from God, but not all the time. I just don't seem to dream very often."

"You're getting them," I replied. "You just haven't been pulling them out of your memory when you wake up."

"You think so?" he asked.

"Yes, that's usually the way it is. People forget to recall their dreams when they first awaken. Try it tonight and see what happens."

We left it at that. While we were sharing breakfast the next morning, I asked, "Did you get a dream last night?"

"As a matter of fact, I did!" he enthusiastically responded. He shared his dream and even some of its interpretation with me. The dream gave him some valuable insight about his relationship with the Lord.

The next morning, as he drove me to the airport to catch my flight, I asked, "Did you get a dream last night?"

"As a matter of fact, I did!" he replied. His enthusiasm bubbled over as he conveyed what God had shown him. He was beginning to get into the flow.

This scenario often repeats itself. I remind people to pull a dream out of their memory when they wake up, and sure enough, the dream is there. Every time this has happened, the dream has proven to be anointed counsel in the night season.

Another pastor and his wife recently hosted me in their home. As we discussed dreams, their story was similar. She got dreams fairly often; he got one occasionally. They were not writing their dreams down. Both of them had taken my teaching course.

"Let's see what happens tonight," I suggested. Both of them received dreams from God that very night. Both of them lost most of their respective dreams, however, because they didn't write them down. This couple remembered just enough of their dreams to know they were from God. As they awakened, both of them thought, I know this is from God; I need to remember it.

Would you believe it? The very same thing happened the next night. I went out that day and bought each of them a composition book so they could record their dreams.

Make the Investment

These examples are fairly typical. Hearing from God in the night season requires genuine determination and effort to get into the flow. Perhaps I didn't emphasize this factor enough in my seminars. On the other hand, some of my staff and other congregation members have pressed in and constantly hear from God in the night season.

At the close of my seminars I tell people that developing this means of hearing from God is like anything else.

It takes effort.

It takes self-discipline.

It requires some of your time and energy.

Recording and studying your dreams on a consistent basis take persistence, determination, and discipline. Your diligence will be rewarded. God has promised that *"he who sows sparingly will also reap sparingly, and he who sows bountifully will also reap bountifully"* (2 Corinthians 9:6). The benefit that you derive from it will be directly proportional to the time and effort that you invest.

Hearing from God in the night season is like learning how to play tennis or golf. It's like learning how to play the piano or the guitar. I suppose you could say that hearing from God in dreams is like anything else in life. What you put into it is exactly what you will get out of it. Doesn't that make sense? After all, everything in life seems to follow this same pattern.

I give this advice to everyone, but especially to those who are in full-time ministry. Please do not neglect developing this important channel of hearing from God. It can be immensely important to you in days to come.

Do not underrate the importance of developing your skill in this key area. You need to hear from God in these last days! Develop your skill in hearing from Him in all of the ways He speaks—including dreams!

The night season can become a very important part of your spiritual life. God can talk to you about your business, your finances, your family, your marriage, your decisions, your ministry, and all aspects of your life in the night season.

It's up to you! The potential benefits of hearing from God even while you sleep are immeasurable. Get serious about hearing from God—even in dreams. It can pay you big dividends and help you avoid costly mistakes. Hearing from God can make a world of difference in your life.

I've done my best to share with you what I've learned about the exciting world of dreams. I've enjoyed the tour.

I wish you many more journeys into this fascinating land. May each one help you to reap treasures of guidance and knowledge from God as my journeys have for me. May you be in tune with God like never before in these end times, including hearing from Him in the night season.

What more can I say?

Except, perhaps...bon voyage and sweet dreams!

FINAL WORDS

In order for the principles on receiving and interpreting dreams to fully operate in your life, you must be born again and baptized in the Holy Spirit. These steps are necessary to walk in all the fullness that God has for you.

Have you received Jesus as your Lord and Savior? If you've never turned from your sin and prayed, "Jesus, I want You to come into my life and be my Savior," then you don't have eternal life. You will have to pay for your sins. And do you know what the payment is? The Bible says that *"the wages of sin is death"* (Romans 6:23). You can suffer the punishment for your sins or you can accept Jesus' death as payment for them. The Gospel is that simple.

You don't have to face eternal torment. You can be at peace with God through Jesus Christ. Ask Him now to forgive you of your sins and to come into your heart. You can pray this simple prayer:

Dear Lord Jesus,

I entrust my life to You. I give You my past, my present, and my future. I turn from all the sins I've committed. I believe that You died in my place and that Your blood washes away my sins forever. I believe that God raised You from the dead so that I can have eternal life with You.

Come into my heart and give me a new life. Teach me by Your Word and by the Holy Spirit. Keep me from following the lies of the devil. Thank You, Lord, for saving me. Help me to live for You. In Jesus' name I pray. Amen.

Welcome to God's family! You will spend eternity with God in heaven. Scripture says,

> *God has given us eternal life, and this life is in His Son. He who has the Son has life; he who does not have the Son does not have life. These things I have written to you who believe in the name of the Son of God, that you may know that you have eternal life.* (1 John 5:11–13)

I encourage you to find a Bible-believing church where you can grow in your faith. Read the Bible daily and talk to God in prayer. Tell someone what Jesus has just done for you.

If you haven't been baptized with the Holy Spirit, you don't have to wait any longer. This tremendous scriptural experience equips the believer with power to witness. The baptism in the Holy Spirit also unleashes spiritual gifts in the believer's life. (See 1 Corinthians 12,14.) Many Christians find that after they receive this baptism, they hear from God more clearly —even in the night season. What did Jesus say about this experience?

> *And being assembled together with them, He [Jesus] commanded them not to depart from Jerusalem, but to wait for the Promise of the Father, "which," He said, "you have heard from Me; for John truly baptized with water, but you shall be baptized with the Holy Spirit not many days from now.... You shall receive power when the Holy Spirit has come upon you; and you shall be witnesses to Me in Jerusalem, and in all*

Judea and Samaria, and to the end of the earth."

(Acts 1:4–5. 8)

After Jesus ascended into heaven, the disciples gathered to wait for the promise of the Holy Spirit. When the day of Pentecost came, *"they were all filled with the Holy Spirit and began to speak with other tongues, as the Spirit gave them utterance"* (Acts 2:4).

How can you know this experience is for today and not just the first century church? When Peter preached to the Jews who were assembled in Jerusalem on the day of Pentecost he said:

Repent, and let every one of you be baptized in the name of Jesus Christ for the remission of sins; and you shall receive the gift of the Holy Spirit. For the promise is to you and to your children, and to all who are afar off, as many as the Lord our God will call. (Acts 2:38–39)

Wouldn't you agree that we are those who are *"afar off"*? Two thousand years separate us from that initial outpouring of the Holy Spirit, but God says the promise is for us, too!

If you've received Jesus as your Lord and Savior, you're ready to receive the baptism with the Holy Spirit. It only takes a moment to ask in faith and receive this gift from God. Simply ask the Lord Jesus to baptize you. Believe that you'll be endued with power from God and that you'll be able to speak with other tongues. Pray this prayer:

Lord Jesus,

The Bible says that You baptize with the Holy Spirit and with fire. I ask you to baptize me right now and give me a heavenly language. I thank You, Lord, and believe that I can speak with other tongues. Amen.

Don't worry about sounding foolish. Begin to pray in faith, expecting an unknown language to spill from your lips. That's your prayer language. Scripture says, *"For if I pray in a tongue, my spirit prays"* (1 Corinthians 14:14). Praying in tongues bypasses your natural reasoning and intellect.

Scripture also says, *"I will pray with the spirit, and I will also pray with the understanding. I will sing with the spirit, and I will also sing with the understanding"* (1 Corinthians 14:15). Read Acts and 1 Corinthians to understand more about your experience.

Don't be surprised if you begin to see supernatural events occur in your life. You've just embarked on an exciting adventure in the Holy Spirit!

ABOUT THE AUTHOR

Benny Thomas is an internationally known Bible teacher and author who has been in the traveling ministry for over 35 years. His tours take him throughout the United States and into foreign countries each year, conducting impartation conferences and other meetings, and making frequent appearances on Christian radio and television.

His unique style of teaching blends practical application and life-changing revelation, which brings believers into a higher level of walking in the Spirit, hearing God's voice, and finding and fulfilling their assignments in the kingdom of God. His ministry is a prophetic one, accompanied by the operation of the gifts of the Holy Spirit, including prophecy, words of knowledge, gifts of healings, and working of miracles.

He is also Senior Pastor of Church of Living Waters in Beaumont, Texas, where he and his wife, Sandy, oversee the church; a ministry training school, LogosRhema Training International; and Benny Thomas Ministries. Additional information about his ministry and teaching materials can be obtained by visiting his website, www.bennythomas.org., or by writing him at Benny Thomas Ministries, P.O. Box 7820, Beaumont, Texas, 77726.